MAX REGER

ZWÖLF STÜCKE

TWELVE PIECES

Opus 59

für Orgel / for Organ

Herausgegeben von / Edited by
Martin Schmeding

ALLE RECHTE VORBEHALTEN · ALL RIGHTS RESERVED
EDITION PETERS
PUBLISHED BY FABER MUSIC
Leipzig · London · New York

This edition © 2024 Faber Music Ltd
Brownlow Yard, 12 Roger Street, London WC1N 2JU
Printed in England by Caligraving Ltd
Alle Rechte vorbehalten · All rights reserved
Vervielfältigungen jeglicher Art sind gesetzlich verboten.
Any unauthorized reproduction is prohibited by law.

ISMN 979-0-014-13513-3

INHALT / CONTENTS

Vorwort / Preface .... IV / V
Anmerkungen zur Aufführungspraxis / Performance Notes VII

Heft 1 / Vol. I

1. Praeludium 2
2. Pastorale 8
3. Intermezzo 11
4. Canon 16
5. Toccata 18
6. Fuge 23

Heft 2 / Vol. II

7. Kyrie eleison 30
8. Gloria in excelsis 34
9. Benedictus 40
10. Capriccio 44
11. Melodia 50
12. Te Deum 54

Anhang: Die von Karl Straube eingerichteten Sätze 5–9 /
Appendix: The arranged settings 5–9 by Karl Straube

5a. Toccata 60
6a. Fuge 65
7a. Kyrie eleison 71
8a. Gloria in excelsis 76
9a. Benedictus 82

Kritischer Bericht / Critical Commentary 87

VORWORT

Mit dem Jahr 1897 spitzte sich Regers private und berufliche Situation immer mehr zu: Seine Stücke erfuhren zum Teil heftige Ablehnung, auch sein Verleger George Augener kehrte sich von ihm ab, und zahlreiche Musiker und Personen des öffentlichen Lebens sahen in ihm das gescheiterte Genie.

Vorausgegangen war eine katastrophale Zeit als Einjährig-Freiwilliger im Militärdienst, die ihn gesundheitlich und finanziell in den Ruin führte und mehrere Lazarettaufenthalte erforderlich machte.

Schließlich konnte ihn seine jüngere Schwester Emma zur Heimkehr in sein Elternhaus nach Weiden bewegen, wo er sich grundsätzlich regenerieren sollte. Wie befreit vom existenziellen Druck und unter dem Einfluss intensiver Lektüre der zeitgenössischen Literatur wird diese Lebensphase die für die Orgelkomposition produktivste und aufregendste werden: „Die Kompositionen wachsen wie das reinste Unkraut."[1]

Im Zentrum des Orgelschaffens stehen in den Weidener Jahren die von Reger selbst als „meine Elefanten"[2] bezeichneten Großwerke: *Fantasie und Fuge über B-A-C-H* op. 46, die *Symphonische Fantasie und Fuge* op. 57 und die Choralfantasien. Den Kritiken wegen immenser spieltechnischer Schwierigkeiten und zu großer Komplexität begegnete er mit folgenden Worten: „Ich kann mit bestem Willen meine Ansprüche an die Ausführenden, meine Schreibweise nicht aufgeben, will ich das erreichen, was mir künstlerisch vorschwebt."[3]

Mit dem Erstarken seiner Gesundheit stellte sich jedoch allmählich auch Max Regers Bedürfnis nach Öffentlichkeit und Anerkennung ein, und er erwies sich immer mehr als Pragmatiker. Da die monumentalen Orgelwerke von zahlreichen Organisten als „unspielbar" bezeichnet wurde, bemühte er sich in den Folgejahren und vor allem mit seiner Übersiedlung nach München um die Komposition leichter fassbarer und aufführbarer Orgelwerke.

Für Max Reger bedeutete die erste Sammlung kürzerer Orgelstücke eine Umstellung in der Arbeits- und Herangehensweise. Adalbert Lindner, sein erster Lehrer, berichtet darüber: „Die sämtlichen zwölf Stücke hat der Meister in vierzehn Tagen geschrieben. Jeden Abend (sonntags ausgenommen) brachte er mir ein druckreif geschriebenes Stück und dazu den mir jedesmal als Geschenk überlassenen Bogen der ersten Niederschrift, den ich mit dem betreffenden Datum versah, Nr. 1 trägt den 17. Juni 1901."[4]

Am Ende einiger Nummern des skizzenhaften Entwurfs sind Entstehungsdaten notiert:

Nr. 1 Praeludium e-Moll: 17.06.1901

Nr. 2 Pastorale F-Dur: 18.06.1901

Nr. 3 Intermezzo a-Moll: 18.06.1901

Nr. 4 Canon E-Dur: 19.06.1901

Nr. 5 Toccata d-Moll: 20.06.1901

Nr. 9 Benedictus Des-Dur: 26.06.1901

Nr. 12 Te Deum a-Moll: „vollendet 1.7.1901. In 14 Tagen geschrieben"

Der Peters-Verlag, der an die Stelle des Londoner Verlegers Augener trat, hatte um eine Folge von mittelschweren Orgelstücken gebeten (nachdem die Monumentalwerke kurz zuvor noch kategorisch abgelehnt worden waren). In einem Brief vom 31. Mai 1901 schrieb Reger an Henri Hinrichsen, den Inhaber des Verlags C. F. Peters: „Die Herren Hug werden Ihnen mitgetheilt haben, daß ich sehr gerne bereit bin für Ihren hochgeschätzten Verlag eine Reihe von mittelschweren Stücken für die Orgel zu schreiben; [...] Die Stücke sind alle nicht schwer technisch; u. erhalten Sie mein vollständig druckfertiges Manuskript bis Ende July, spätestens Anfang August dieses Jahres."[5]

Wenn Max Reger mit der Übersendung des Manuskriptes am 13. Juli 1901 die Nr. 2, 4, 9 und 11 jedoch als allerleichtest charakterisiert, dann liegt darin wohl auch Koketterie. Nachdem die Korrekturen bis zum 9. August vollendet waren, erhielt Reger bis Anfang September die fertigen Druckexemplare.

Zumindest die Verkaufs- und Auflagenzahlen weisen eindrücklich die Beliebtheit dieser ersten Sammlung von Charakterstücken nach, bis 1918 erscheinen insgesamt sieben Auflagen sowie Regers Bearbeitung des Benedictus für Harmonium (1908) und die Einrichtung Karl Straubes der Nr. 7–9 (1912) bzw. der Toccata und Fuge d-Moll / D-Dur im Sammelband von „Präludien und Fugen" (1919). Auch die den großen Orgelwerken der Weidener Zeit skeptisch gegenüber eingestellte Presse reagiert erfreut: „Vergleicht man diese Stücke op. 59 mit den drei aus op. 52, so läßt sich eine wunderbare Klärung der ganzen Mache den letzteren gegenüber konstatiren, wobei trotzdem der gesammte Kunstapparat in gleicher Vollendung funktioniert. Diese Orgelstücke Op. 59 sind wahre Fundgruben von Schönheiten für jeden perfekten Orgelspieler und sie werden überall ihr begeistertes Publikum finden."[6]

---

[1] Brief vom 9. Februar 1899 an Jacob Johannes Baron von Fridagh, zit. nach: Susanne Popp (Hg.), *Der junge Reger*, Wiesbaden 2000, S. 386.

[2] Brief vom 14. Januar 1901 an Otto Leßmann, Max-Reger-Institut, Ep. Ms. 185

[3] Brief vom 1. Mai 1900 an Alexander Wilhelm Gottschalg, Meininger Museen, Max-Reger-Archiv, Br 034/9.

[4] Notiz Adalbert Lindners als Beilage der Mappe mit den Entwurf-Manuskripten, Stadtmuseum Weiden, Sign. C5.

[5] Brief vom 31. Mai 1901 an Henri Hinrichsen, zit. nach: S. Popp und S. Shigihara (Hg.), *Max Reger – Briefwechsel mit dem Verlag C. F. Peters*, Bonn 1995, S. 46.

[6] Heinrich Lang, Rezension in der Allgemeinen Musik-Zeitung 28. Jg. (1901), Nr. 49, S. 800.

PREFACE

Mit den *Zwölf Stücken* op. 59 legt Reger ein Kompendium der historischen und zeitgenössischen Formen dar: In Präludium (Nr. 1), Canon (Nr. 4), Toccata (Nr. 5) und Fuge (Nr. 6) greift er auf die barocken Formvorbilder zurück, wobei die Fuge als grandiose dynamische und tempomäßige Steigerung angelegt ist. Des Weiteren enthält der Zyklus mit den Sätzen Kyrie eleison (Nr. 7), Gloria in excelsis (Nr. 8), Benedictus (Nr. 10) und Te Deum (Nr. 12) ein Repertoire für das katholische Mess-Ordinarium – vielleicht ein Ausgleich zu den ansonsten dominierenden, protestantischen Chorälen in Regers Orgelschaffen. Als letzte Gruppe sind mit Pastorale (Nr. 2), Intermezzo (Nr. 3), Capriccio (Nr. 10) und Melodia (Nr. 11) die romantischen Charakterstücke vertreten, wie sie auch aus zahlreichen kürzeren, eigenen Klavierwerken bekannt sind.

Immer wiederkehrendes, charakteristisches Element der kleineren Orgelwerke ist die dreiteilige Form mit variierter Reprise und kontrastierend angelegtem Mittelteil. Die wechselnden Stimmungen entsprechen Lindners Charakterisierung von Regers kompositorischen Kennzeichen in das Trotzig-Titanisch-Dämonische, das Humoristisch-Burleske und das Innige. Einige der Werke, wie z.B. die Toccata d-Moll werden zu den am häufigsten aufgeführten Orgelwerken Regers. Das Benedictus in seiner verklärten Stimmung wird in der Literatur als eines der schönsten und innigsten Werke des Komponisten bezeichnet.

In den Jahren 1912 („mit Einwilligung des Komponisten") und 1919 legte Regers Freund und Interpret Karl Straube, Orgelprofessor am Leipziger Königlichen Konservatorium der Musik und Thomasorganist bzw. Thomaskantor Nr. 5–9 in einer eigenen Ausführungsfassung vor, die interessante Einblicke in eine mögliche Interpretationspraxis gibt, aber auch Kontroversen hervorruft. Deswegen soll in der vorliegenden Ausgabe der nach den Quellen überarbeitete Urtext Max Regers zusammen mit dem Nachdruck der Bearbeitungen Straubes als Grundlage einer aufführungspraktischen Betrachtung und Diskussion präsentiert werden. Daraus können sich für die heutige Interpretation spannende und neuartige Ansatzpunkte ergeben.

Leipzig, Juni 2024 *Martin Schmeding*

In 1897, Reger's private and professional issues came to a head: his pieces were in part violently rejected, his publisher George Augener turned his back on him, and numerous musicians and public figures regarded him as a failed genius.

This was preceded by a disastrous time as a one-year volunteer in military service, which ruined both his health and financial situation and necessitated several hospitalisations.

In the end, his younger sister Emma was able to persuade him to return to his parents' house in Weiden, where he supposedly recovered. As if freed from existential pressure and influenced by intensive reading of contemporary literature, this phase of his life was to be the most productive and exciting for organ composition: 'The compositions grew like the purest weeds.'[1]

At the centre of Reger's organ output in the Weiden years are the large-scale works that Reger himself described as 'my elephants'[2]: *Fantasia and Fugue on B-A-C-H* Op. 46, the *Symphonic Fantasia and Fugue* Op. 57 and the Choral Fantasies. He responded to the criticism of immense technical difficulties and excessive complexity with the following words: 'With the best will in the world, I cannot give up my demands on the performers and my way of writing, if I want to achieve what I have in mind artistically.'[3]

As his health improved, Reger's need for publicity and recognition gradually materialized; he also proved himself to be more and more of a pragmatist. As the monumental organ works were labelled 'unplayable' by numerous organists, he endeavoured to compose organ works that were easier to grasp and perform in the years that followed, especially when he moved to Munich.

For Max Reger, the first collection of shorter organ pieces signalled a change in his working method and approach. Adalbert Lindner, his first teacher, reported: 'The master wrote all twelve pieces in a fortnight. Every evening (except Sundays) he brought me a piece that was ready for printing, along with the sheet of the first manuscript that he gave me as a gift each time, which I marked with the relevant date. No. 1 is dated 17 June 1901.'[4]

The dates of composition are noted at the end of some numbers of the sketchy draft:

No. 1 Prelude in E minor: 17 June 1901

No. 2 Pastorale in F major: 18 June 1901

No. 3 Intermezzo in A minor: 18 June 1901

No. 4 Canon in E major: 19 June 1901

No. 5 Toccata in D minor: 20 June 1901

No. 9 Benedictus in D flat major: 26 June 1901

No. 12 Te Deum in A minor: 'completed 1 July 1901, written in 14 days'

---

[1] Letter from 9 February 1899 to Jacob Johannes Baron von Fridagh, quoted by Susanne Popp (ed.), *Der junge Reger*, Wiesbaden 2000, p. 386.

[2] Letter from 14 January 1901 to Otto Leßmann, Max-Reger-Institut, Ep. Ms. 185.

[3] Letter from 1 May 1900 to Alexander Wilhelm Gottschalg, Meininger Museen, Max-Reger-Archiv, Br 034/9.

[4] Note by Adalbert Lindner as attachment of the collection with drafted manuscripts, Stadtmuseum Weiden, shelf mark: C5.

The publisher C. F. Peters, who took the place of the London publisher Augener, had asked for a series of organ pieces of medium difficulty (the monumental works had been categorically rejected shortly before). In a letter dated 31 May 1901, he wrote to Henri Hinrichsen, the owner of the publishing house C. F. Peters: 'The gentlemen Hug will have informed you that I am very happy to write a series of pieces of <u>medium difficulty</u> for the organ for your highly esteemed publishing house; [...] All of the pieces are <u>not</u> technically difficult; and you will receive my complete manuscript ready for printing by the end of July, at the latest at the beginning of August this year.'[5]

However, when Max Reger characterised Nos. 2, 4, 9 and 11 as the easiest when he sent the manuscript on 13 July 1901, it must have been with a certain degree of humour. After the corrections had been completed by 9 August, Reger received the finished printed copies by the beginning of September.

The sales and print run figures impressively demonstrate the popularity of this first collection of character pieces, with a total of seven editions appearing by 1918, as well as Reger's arrangement of the Benedictus for harmonium (1908) and Karl Straube's arrangement of Nos. 7–9 (1912) and the Toccata and Fugue in D minor / D major in the anthology of 'Preludes and Fugues' (1919).

Even the press, which was sceptical about the great organ works of the Weiden period, reacted with delight: 'If one compares these pieces Op. 59 with the three from Op. 52, one can see a wonderful clarification of the entire compositional process, although the artistic apparatus still functions with the same perfection. These organ pieces Op. 59 are a real treasure trove of beauty for all organists and they will find an enthusiastic audience everywhere.'[6]

With the *Twelve Pieces* Op. 59, Reger presents a compendium of historical and contemporary forms: in Prelude (No. 1), Canon (No. 4), Toccata (No. 5) and Fugue (No. 6), he draws on Baroque formal models, whereby the fugue is designed with a grandiose dynamic and tempo increase. Furthermore, the cycle contains repertoire for the catholic Mass Ordinary with the movements Kyrie eleison (No. 7), Gloria in excelsis (No. 8), Benedictus (No. 10) and Te Deum (No. 12) – perhaps a counterbalance to the dominance of Protestant chorales in Reger's organ works otherwise. The last group, Pastorale (No. 2), Intermezzo (No. 3), Capriccio (No. 10) and Melodia (No. 11), are Romantic character pieces, which are also recognisable from numerous of his own shorter piano works.

A recurring, characteristic element of the smaller organ works is the three-part form with a varied recapitulation and contrasting middle section. The changing moods correspond to Lindner's characterisation of Reger's compositional hallmarks as defiantly titanic-demonic, humorous-burlesque and intimate. Some of the works, such as the Toccata in D minor, are among Reger's most frequently performed. The Benedictus in its transfigured mood is considered one of the composer's most beautiful and heartfelt works.

In 1912 ('with the composer's consent') and 1919, Reger's friend and interpreter Karl Straube, organ professor at the Leipzig Royal Conservatory of Music and organist and cantor at St Thomas's, presented his own version of Nos. 5–9, which provides interesting insights into a possible interpretation, but also provokes controversy. For this reason, this edition presents Max Reger's Urtext, revised according to the sources, together with the reprint of Straube's arrangements as a basis for practical performance considerations and discussions. This can give rise to exciting and novel starting points for modern interpretation.

Leipzig, June 2024 *Martin Schmeding*

---

[5] Letter from vom 31 May 1901 to Henri Hinrichsen, quoted following S. Popp and S. Shigihara (ed.), *Max Reger – Briefwechsel mit dem Verlag C. F. Peters*, Bonn 1995, p. 46.
[6] Heinrich Lang, review in the *Allgemeine Musik-Zeitung* 28 (1901), No. 49, p. 800.

ANMERKUNGEN ZUR AUFFÜHRUNGSPRAXIS / PERFORMANCE NOTES

Zur Aufführung der Orgelwerke Regers

In den vergangenen hundert Jahren seit Regers Tod hat der vollständige Wandel in Gesellschaft, Musikästhetik, Orgelbau und Aufführungspraxis zu einem weitgehenden Verlust einer kontinuierlichen Interpretationstradition seiner Werke geführt.

Max Reger hat seine Autografe mit zahlreichen Anmerkungen zu Dynamik, Tempo, Registrierung, Phrasierung und Artikulation versehen, oft in mehrfarbiger Schrift. Ausführliche Korrekturen zeugen an vielen Stellen von der Intensität und Genauigkeit der Auseinandersetzung des Komponisten mit aufführungspraktischen Fragen.

Dass seine Schreibweise an die Grenzen des zu seiner Zeit Machbaren geht, bekennt er selbst in einem Brief an den befreundeten Organisten Gustav Beckmann: „Meine Orgelsachen sind schwer, es gehört ein über die Technik souverän herrschender geistvoller Spieler dazu […]. Man macht mir oft den Vorwurf, dass ich absichtlich so schwer schreibe; gegen diesen Vorwurf habe ich nur eine Antwort, dass keine Note zuviel darin steht."[1] Neben dem Notentext sind auch die Ausführungsanweisungen als essentiell zu betrachten.

In einigen Kommentaren bietet Reger selbst Lösungen für praktische Probleme an, z. B. in Bezug auf die Tempowahl: „Ich bitte alle Metronomangaben nicht strikte bindend anzusehen; doch dürften die Metronomangaben besonders bei den bewegten (schnellen) Variationen und hauptsächlich bei der Fuge, der ein breites Tempo gelegen sein wird, als die überhaupt höchst zulässigen Tempi in Bezug auf ‚Schnelligkeit' gelten, wenn nicht der Vortrag auf Kosten der Deutlichkeit leiden soll."[2]

Was sein Freund und Interpret Karl Straube in seinen Notenausgaben manchmal mit dem Wort „flessibile" andeutet, beschreibt Reger für die Ausführung von Johann Sebastian Bachs Werken – und somit indirekt auch für seine eigenen Kompositionen: „Bitte spielen Sie Bach nie nach Metronom, sondern wie es Ihnen ums Herz ist […]. Vor allem muß beim Bachspiel das Tempo so genommen werden, daß jede Figur ausdrucksvoll wird; in Folge dessen nehmen Sie ganz ruhig Ihre Tempi!"[3]

Hinsichtlich der Kritik an den Vortragsanweisungen Regers geht jedoch Karl Straube, der als Orgelprofessor am Leipziger Königlichen Konservatorium der Musik ganze Schülergenerationen ausbildete und damit auch die Reger-Interpretation prägte, noch weiter: „Die rechten Worte und Zeichen festzulegen, die einem Dritten die Möglichkeit gaben, einzudringen in diese geheimnisvolle Tonwelt, das war ihm unmöglich."[4]

Straubes Prinzipien sind über eigene Eintragungen in den Handexemplaren, Notizen in den Noten seiner Schüler und Editionen der Werke Regers (und anderer Komponisten) erhalten. Sie zeigen teilweise erhebliche Eingriffe in die originalen Anweisungen. Als Grundsatz hält er fest: „Die in sich ruhende Einheit des Ganzen muß gewahrt bleiben. Das gleiche gilt für die wechselnden Zeitmaße, die untereinander ausgeglichen werden

---

[1] Max Reger, Brief an Gustav Beckmann vom 10. Januar 1900, zit. nach Alexander Becker et al., *Max Reger. Zwölf Stücke op. 59*, Heft 1, Reger-Werkausgabe, Stuttgart 2011.
[2] Siehe Fußnote 1.
[3] Susanna Popp, *Max Reger. Werk statt Leben*, Wiesbaden 2015, S. 347.
[4] Karl Straube, *Briefe eines Thomaskantors*, Stuttgart 1952, S. 174.

On the performance of Reger's organ works

In the hundred years since Reger's death, the complete change in society, musical aesthetics, organ building and performance practice has led to a far-reaching loss of a continuous interpretative tradition of his works.

Max Reger included numerous annotations on dynamics, tempo, registration, phrasing and articulation on his autograph manuscripts, often in multi-coloured script. In many places, detailed corrections bear witness to the intensity and precision with which the composer dealt with practical performance issues.

He himself admits in a letter to his friend and organist Gustav Beckmann that his style of writing pushed the boundaries of what was possible in his day: 'My organ pieces are difficult, they require a quick-witted player with a commanding technical facility. […] I am often reproached for deliberately writing such difficult music; I have only one answer to this reproach, namely that there is not one note too many.'[1] In addition to the musical text, the performance instructions should also be regarded as essential.

In some commentaries, Reger himself offers solutions to practical problems, e.g. with regard to the choice of tempo: 'I ask that all metronome markings not be regarded as strictly binding; however, the metronome markings should be regarded as the highest permissible tempi in terms of "speed", especially in the moving (fast) variations and especially in the fugue, which will be suited to a broad tempo, if the performance is not to suffer at the expense of clarity.'[2]

What his friend and interpreter Karl Straube sometimes indicated in his editions with the word 'flessibile', Reger described for the performance of Johann Sebastian Bach's works – and thus indirectly also for his own compositions: 'Please never play Bach according to the metronome, but as you feel […]. Above all, when playing Bach, the tempo must be taken in such a way that every figure becomes expressive; as a result, take your tempi very calmly!'[3]

However, Karl Straube, who as organ professor at the Leipzig Royal Conservatory of Music trained entire generations of students and thus also shaped Reger's interpretation, goes even further in his critique of Reger's performance instructions: 'It was impossible for him to determine the right words and signs that would allow a third party to penetrate this mysterious world of sound.'[4]

Straube's principles have been preserved through his own entries in the manuscript copies, notes in his pupils' scores and editions of Reger's works (and those of other composers). Some of them show considerable interventions in the original instructions. As a principle, he states: 'The unity of the whole must be preserved. The same applies to the changing time signatures, which must be balanced out and never lapse into extremes. In all his

---

[1] Max Reger, Brief to Gustav Beckmann from 10 January 1900, quoted following Alexander Becker et al., *Max Reger. Zwölf Stücke op. 59*, vol. 1, Reger Collected Works, (Stuttgart, 2011).
[2] See footnote 1.
[3] Susanna Popp, *Max Reger. Werk statt Leben*, (Wiesbaden, 2015), p. 347.
[4] Karl Straube, *Briefe eines Thomaskantors*, (Stuttgart, 1952), p. 174.

performance indications, both dynamic and agogic, Reger indulged in such intemperance that his indications created more confusion than clarity for non-thinking people. What he wanted to achieve with his *Adagissimi, Vivacissimi, molto agitato, piu molto agitato, Andante (Quasi Allegro vivace)*, never too prominent, with the whole range from pppp to fff, was a soul-stirring performance. The use of train-like tempos or high-pressure siren wails is a crime against his art. The same applies to the opposite of snail-like slowness and inaudible whispering.'[5]

Straube sees the justification for this approach as the will of the composer himself, whose interpretation showed 'with what subtlety of feeling the threatening ffff or pppp were resolved and spiritualised by the composer's hands, so that a perfect unity […] was revealed. Above all, it was a transitional dynamic that was applied; furthermore, in contrast to the exaggerated metronome markings, the time signatures were kept surprisingly moderate and balanced.'[6]

Straube's communication with publishers regarding manuscripts that were submitted without the composer's knowledge, his harsh criticism and the pressure he applied to change compositions, which led Elsa Reger to speak of Straube's 'corrosive spirit'[7], do all suggest that he may have gone too far in his influence over Reger.

The present edition combines the critically reviewed musical text of the *Twelve Pieces* Op. 59, first published in 1901 by C. F. Peters Leipzig, with the arrangement by Karl Straube in the 1912 edition (nos. 7–9, EP 3286) and 1919 edition (nos. 5–6, EP 3008G) and includes performance notes and critical commentary. Together this provides essential starting points for a Reger interpretation based on the original musical text and analysis of contemporary sources. While the later edition was published after Reger's death, the title page of the 1912 publication bears the note 'published in agreement with the composer'.

Reger's original performance instructions

Throughout his compositional activity, Max Reger included practical performance instructions of varying intensity and precision in the musical text.

The central starting point of his thinking was the principles of his teacher Hugo Riemann, which he exemplified in his chorale prelude 'Komm, süßer Tod' WoO IV/3[8] with regard to the agogic structure.

---

[5] Christoph and Ingrid Held (ed.), *Karl Straube. Wirken und Wirkung*, (Berlin, 1976), p. 104f.
[6] See footnote 5, p. 107.
[7] Susanne Popp (ed.), *Max Reger. Briefe an Fritz Stein*, (Bonn, 1981), p. 193.
[8] Mainz: Schott, 1893, p. 3.

* Das Zeichen ∧ bedeutet eine gelinde Dehnung der Note oder Pause, über der es steht; < u. > haben „dynamische" (Schweller) und „agogische" Bedeutung.
 The sign ∧ means a slight stretching of the note or rest above which it stands; < and > have 'dynamic' (swell pedal) and 'agogic' meanings.

Ansonsten weisen Regers Angaben zur Phrasierung und Artikulation nie die Vollständigkeit auf, die Karl Straube in seiner Ausgabe des zweiten Bandes der Bach-Orgelwerk-Ausgabe im Verlag C. F. Peters erreicht. Dort notierte Straube durchgehend sowohl übergeordnete Phrasierungsbögen für die Architektur des Werkes, als auch kürzere Bögen für die Detailgestaltung.[9]

Elsewhere, Reger's indications of phrasing and articulation never have the completeness that Karl Straube achieves in his edition of the second volume of the Bach organ works published by C. F. Peters. There Straube consistently notes both overarching phrasing slurs for the architecture of the work as well as shorter slurs for the detail.[9]

Letztlich gilt es auch für die heutige Interpretation der Werke Regers, diese Klarheit der Strukturierung zu erreichen, wobei Reger einem auf diesem Weg unterschiedliche Vorgaben macht:

Im Frühwerk *Drei Orgelstücke* op. 7 beschränkt sich Reger auf die dynamische Bandbreite vom Pianissimo (***pp***) bis Fortissimo (***ff***), verzichtet auf Bögen und vermerkt nur allgemeine Angaben (Fußtonzahlen) zu den Registrierungen. Er scheint ein schlichtes, „quasi-barockes" Notenbild erreichen zu wollen, passend zum Charakter der Stücke.

Ultimately, it is important for today's interpretation of Reger's works to achieve this clarity of structure, even though Reger gives us varying guidelines along the way:

In the early work *Three Organ Pieces* Op. 7, Reger restricts himself to the dynamic range from pianissimo (***pp***) to fortissimo (***ff***), dispenses with slurs and only notes general indications (footnote numbers) for the registrations. He seems to have been aiming for a simple, 'quasi-baroque' score, in keeping with the character of the pieces.

---

[9] Notenbeispiel aus *Johann Sebastian Bach. Orgelwerke. Neue Ausgabe*, Leipzig: Peters 1913 (EP 3331), S. 113.

[9] Example from *Johann Sebastian Bach. Orgelwerke. Neue Ausgabe*, (Leipzig: Peters, 1913) (EP 3331), p. 113.

The first *Suite* Op. 16 extends the dynamic range from **ppp** to **fff** and includes the first few instructions on dynamics and agogics with continuation lines.

From the first *Chorale Fantasia on 'Ein' feste Burg ist unser Gott'* Op. 27, Reger utilises the entire range of the volume scale from **pppp** to **ffff**. Only a few characteristic articulation markings appear up to the *Chorale Fantasia on 'Freu dich sehr, o meine Seele!'* Op. 30. In the chorale fantasias, registrations are sometimes indicated specifically or as colour values ('dark, light' etc.) alongside footnote numbers. Dynamic and agogic changes (*cresc./decresc., accel./ritard.*) are mostly labelled precisely with continuation lines by Reger from the *Fantasia and Fugue in C minor* Op. 29 onwards.

The *Fantasia and Fugue on B-A-C-H* Op. 46 represents a turning point in terms of the accuracy of the practical performance instructions: The musical text is provided throughout with predominantly long phrasing slurs and some characteristic motif slurs or articulations; registration indications are given with footnote numbers or colour values.

Reger uses detailed articulation indications primarily in scherzo-like works or fast fugues, but even here only up to a certain point, after which he switches back to long slurs.

The fugue from Opus 46 contains detailed metronome markings for the first time, which Reger also checked and corrected in detail. Concrete tempi can still be found in Opus 59 (Nos. 1–3, 6, 8, 9, 11 and 12), Opus 60 ('Choral', fugue), Opus 63 (Nos. 1, 2, 6, 8, 10), Opus 65 (Nos. 1&2), Opus 80 (No. 2) and then again in the late works Op. 127, 129 and 145. It is striking that the early tempo indications seem to be much too fast or difficult to perform in relation to the note values and the density of the movement, while the designation in Opus 80 presents a transition, after which the tempi of the last works seem realistic or even rather moderate. This may be the result of a change in the composer's psychological disposition. While at the turn of the century he spoke of a 'creative compulsion' ('The compositions grow like the purest weeds'[10]), in the last years of his life, without official duties, he embraced the 'free, Jenaish style'[11] in which Reger purely devote himself to composing.

If one looks at Reger's practical performance indications in the overview, it becomes clear that although he does make detailed designations, he does not keep them constant or consistent. Further study of the various parameters and their classification and realisation is therefore of central importance for the interpretation of his works.

Basic arrangement, registration and dynamics

Max Reger was enthusiastic about the possibilities of the contemporary organ in symphonic style: 'But why do our great organ builders such as Sauer, Walcker, etc. build such magnificent works, such organs equipped with all kinds of refinements? I now want to fully utilise the possibilities offered by these modern organs.'[12]

---

[10] Susanne Popp, *Der junge Reger*, (Wiesbaden, 2000), p. 386.

[11] Susanne Popp, *Max Reger. Werk statt Leben*, (Wiesbaden, 2015), p. 435.

[12] Letter (copy) from Max Reger to Ludwig Thuille, dated 4 December 1899, Bayerische Staatsbibliothek München.

However, as he lacked practical experience at the organ, a fact which he was aware of throughout his life, detailed instructions regarding the implementation on modern organs can seem unrealistic or not very practical. Continuous large-scale dynamic movements cannot be translated literally and certainly cannot be represented continuously with the help of the *crescendo* roll, but must be regarded in the more figurative sense of a gradual increase or attenuation. Manual distributions do not always appear to make sense, the use of couplers is often very late, and special passages are not always emphasized on a separate manual.

In this respect, Karl Straube's arrangements for the Sauer organ (1886–1889/1908) in the Thomaskirche in Leipzig (Nos. 7–9) and the Walcker organ (1887, rebuilt by Sauer in 1907) of the Leipzig Conservatory (Nos. 5 and 6) and the exemplary registrations offer a good insight into the 'workshop' of this Reger interpreter.

At the beginning of each work, Straube presents the initial registration in the manual stops and three free combinations. In most cases, at least two free combinations are indicated for different dynamic starting points, the hand registers and often a further combination for special tone colours.

It is striking that Straube often couples the manuals with each other from the beginning and then achieves tonal differentiation through additional manual changes (cf. here the beginning of Toccata No. 5 in the Straube version[13] as an example). The individual sounds are never chosen schematically, but 'orchestrated' in a typically characteristic manner.

Starting from the initial registrations, dynamic movements are achieved with the help of the roller, a mechanical rolling device for the foot that sequentially introduces the stops. Straube clearly distinguishes its use from the Schweller (dynamic forks) and restricts it to technically 'feasible' passages with regard to the foot movement with simultaneous roller operation.

In the individual numbers there are the following conspicuous features:

No. 5 Toccata

Reger consistently marks the loud passages with *meno **ff** – **ff*** – Org. pl.

Straube differentiates here on the basis of the sequence structure of the beginning ***mp** – **mf** – poco forte* and then only in the further section up to ***ff*** and ***fff***. In accordance with the refined dynamics, he also uses all three manuals with frequent alternation.

In bar 12ff. he distributes the arpeggio structure over two manuals in order to emphasise the latent chromaticism of the lower voice, a typical effect in Straube's settings.

The quiet middle section from bar 21 onwards is 'orchestrated' by changing individual stops. These changes could be carried out by the performer himself, which according to some of Straube's pupils was an important concern of their teacher.

The literal realisation of all of Reger's indications would require the help of one or two assistants – this is where pragmatism and faithfulness to the score meet and must be judged and individually considered.

A completely different picture emerges in bar 33 at the end of the Toccata. While Reger allows the dynamic undulations of the conclusion to merge seamlessly dynamically and

---

[13] See p. 60.

übergehen lässt, setzt Straube *subito* im **pp** und *Adagio* an, vermeidet dadurch technische und klangliche Probleme und steigert erst ab dem Orgelpunkt im Pedal in T. 36 (Reger beginnt schon vermeintlich „zu früh" in der Mitte von T. 35), der sich gut in einem Fuß parallel zur Walzenbedienung spielen lässt.

Nr. 6 Fuge

Hier ist nur die Vorbereitung der Handregister notwendig, was am Schluss der Toccata geschehen kann. Straube erweitert die Steigerung durch den Beginn auf dem dritten Manual. So kann er auch die Manualwechsel in T. 22 und T. 34 (Umkehrung des Themas) an formal wichtigen Positionen einführen. Während Reger schon früh und nahezu durchgehend Tempo und Dynamik steigert, beginnt Straube mit der Addition einzelner Handregister und dem Öffnen des Schwellers. Da er das Werk in unterschiedliche Abschnitte gliedert und damit die sukzessive Tempo-Steigerung übergeht, kann er den Walzengebrauch auf praktikable Momente beschränken. Insgesamt setzt er die dynamischen Ebenen etwas später steigernd an, so dass es zu einer großen Schlussapotheose kommt. Der lineare Steigerungsverlauf wird jedoch in Straubes Version vollständig „geordnet" und somit zerstört.

Nr. 7 Kyrie eleison

Für die leisen Rahmenteile, die durch zahlreiche Wechsel der Klangfarben im „Mikrobereich" gekennzeichnet sind, wählt Straube die Handregister, da diese vom Organisten einfach selbst zu bedienen sind. Aufgrund der speziellen Klangfarbe der Manualakkorde in T. 5 und der solistischen Bassstimme in T. 9 mit anschließender Steigerung, benötigt Straube eine zusätzliche Kombination. Außerdem ignoriert er die für Reger häufig so entscheidende Farbwirkung der begleitenden 8´+4´-Verbindung. Dafür wählt er eine höchst interessante Kombination von Schwebung und Aliquot (*Voix céleste* und *Quinte 2 2/3´*).

Im weiteren Verlauf greift Straube an entscheidender Stelle „ordnend" ein: Während Reger Dynamik und Tempo bis T. 19 durchgehend steigert und dann direkt zurückführt, entkoppelt Straube beide Parameter: Da die Akkordballungen in T. 18 schwer zu greifen sind, verlangsamt er vorher das Tempo und steigert nur die Lautstärke, die dann auch noch länger erhalten bleibt, um einen Choraleffekt in T. 20 zu erreichen. Ebenso ordnet er in den Kontrasttakten 35ff. die Tempoebenen genau proportional im Verhältnis 2:1, während Reger nur „agitato" schreibt. Ob die Vereinheitlichung in Regers Sinn ist, muss stark angezweifelt werden, da sie das musikalische Aufbrausen doch stark vorhersehbar gestaltet.

Nr. 8 Gloria in excelsis

Ähnlich wie in Nr. 5 differenziert Straube den Beginn aus, indem er die Steigerung ab T. 4 im **mf** beginnen lässt und auch das Tempo gegenüber dem choralartigen Beginn erhöht. Für die individuellen Klangfarben der einzelnen Teile nutzt er jeweils eine freie Kombination, um dann mit der Walze zu steigern. Die Fuge ab T. 22 zeigt exemplarisch, wie eine hinsichtlich der Phrasierung durchgestaltete Version aussehen kann. Der langsame Mittelteil wird in Tempo und Dynamik kontrastierend komplett vom Rahmenteil abgesetzt. Wie in vielen Einrichtungen beginnt Straube auch hier das Schluss-Ritardando wesentlich früher.

---

agogically, Straube begins *subito* **pp** and *Adagio*, thereby avoiding technical and tonal problems, and only increases from the organ point in the pedal in bar 36 (Reger already begins supposedly 'too early' in the middle of bar 35), which can be played well in one foot parallel to the roll control.

No. 6 Fuge

Here it is only necessary to prepare the hand stops, which can be done at the end of the Toccata. Straube extends the intensification by beginning on the third manual. This way, he can also introduce the manual changes in bar 22 and 34 (inversion of the theme) at the crucial moments. While Reger increases the tempo and dynamics early on and almost continuously, Straube begins with the addition of individual manual stops and the opening of the swell. As he divides the work into different sections and thus passes over the successive tempo increase, he is able to limit the use of the roll to practicable moments. Overall, he increases the dynamic levels somewhat later, resulting in a large final apotheosis. In Straube's version, however, the linear increase is completely 'organised' and thus deleted.

No. 7 Kyrie eleison

Straube chooses manual stops for the quiet frame sections, which are characterised by numerous changes of tone colour in the 'micro range', as these are easy for the organist to operate himself. Due to the special tone colour of the manual chords in bar 5 and the solo bass part in bar 9 with subsequent intensification, Straube calls for an additional combination. He also ignores the colour effect of the accompanying 8´+4´ connection, which was often so important for Reger. Instead, he chooses a particularly interesting combination of beat and aliquot (*Voix céleste* and *Quinte 2 2/3´*).

During the course of the work, Straube intervenes at specific points to 'get organised'. While Reger continuously increases the dynamics and tempo up to bar 19 and then immediately retreats, Straube decouples the two parameters. As the chordal clusters in bar 18 are difficult to grasp, he slows down the tempo beforehand and only increases the volume, which is then maintained for longer in order to achieve a chorale effect in bar 20. Similarly, in the contrasting bars 35ff. he arranges the tempo levels exactly proportionally in a ratio of 2:1, whereas Reger only writes 'agitato'. Whether this standardisation is in Reger's interest must be highly doubtful, as it makes the musical effervescence very predictable.

No. 8 Gloria in excelsis

Similarly to No. 5, Straube differentiates the beginning by starting the ascent from **mf** in bar 4 and also increasing the tempo compared to the chorale-like beginning. He uses a free combination for the individual tonal colours of the individual sections and then increases them with the roll. The fugue from bar 22 onwards is a good example of how a version with carefully crafted phrasing can look. The slow middle section is set apart from the frame section by the contrasting tempo and dynamics. As in many settings, Straube also begins the final *ritardando* much earlier here.

Nr. 9 Benedictus

Bemerkenswert sind zunächst die detailliert orchestrierten, aparten Streicherfarben des Beginns. Mit dem sehr diskret verinnerlichten Klang korrespondiert eine im Vergleich zum Original kleingliedrigere Abstufung der Feindynamik. Zur Verstärkung der Crescendo-Wirkung beginnt Straube den Mittelteil im **mp** statt **mf**. Während Reger die Steigerung bis zum Orgelpunkt in T. 46 fortführt, bremst Straube das Tempo schon ab Beginn der Sequenz T. 40. Dieser Eingriff erscheint gegenüber der rastlosen Steigerungswirkung des Originals als starke Änderung der Intention des Komponisten.

Phrasierung und Artikulation

Max Regers Lehrer Hugo Riemann sieht im auftaktigen Denken die kleinstmögliche musikalische Einheit – durchaus im Kontrast zur barocken Lehre von Thesis–Arsis bzw. guter und schlechter Zählzeit im Sinne eines Schwer/leicht-Decrescendos.

No. 9 Benedictus

First of all, the detailed orchestration and distinctive string colours at the beginning are remarkable. The somewhat internalized sound is a result of the more subtle gradation of the dynamics compared to the original. To increase the *crescendo* effect, Straube begins the middle section **mp** instead of **mf**. While Reger continues the increase up to the organ point in bar 46, Straube slows down the tempo from the beginning of the sequence in bar 40. This intervention appears to be an obvious change to the composer's intention and the increasingly restless effect of the original.

Phrasing and articulation

Max Reger's teacher Hugo Riemann saw the subtlest musical possibilities when considering upbeats – in stark contrast to the Baroque doctrine of Thesis–Arsis, or good and bad beats, in the sense of a heavy/light *decrescendo*.

Max Reger, *Passacaglia d-Moll* WoO IV/6, Beginn, mit ergänzter Dynamik (nach Hugo Riemann) / *incipit with added dynamics (foll. Hugo Riemann)*

Aus der Kombination dieser Elemente entstehen drei Arten von Phrasen, die Riemann als „in-, an- und abbetont" kennzeichnet:

Inbetont: <>
Anbetont: >
Abbetont: <

Wie eine ideale Phrasierungs- und Artikulationsbezeichnung eines Notentextes aussehen könnte, hat Straube in seiner Ausgabe des zweiten Bandes der Bach-Orgelwerke[14] exemplarisch gezeigt, wie eingangs bereits erörtert wurde.

Max Reger hat sich in den Orgelwerken nur selten Zeit für eine vollständige Bezeichnung genommen. Häufig setzte er nur sehr lange Phrasierungsbögen und bezeichnete an charakteristischen Stellen spezifische Artikulationen.

Einen direkten Einblick in Regers „Phrasierungswerkstatt" bekommt man, wenn man die nahezu unbezeichnete Orgelfassung der *Choralfantasie über „Freu' dich sehr, o meine Seele!"* op. 30 mit der zeitgleich entstandenen, in zahlreichen Details ausgestalteten Fassung für Klavier vierhändig vergleicht. Grundsätzlich lassen sich folgende Prinzipien und Gedanken in der Bogensetzung feststellen:

The combination of these elements results in three types of phrases, which Riemann characterises as 'in-, at- and de-emphasized':

In-emphasized: <>
At-emphasized: >
De-emphasized: <

In his edition of the second volume of Bach's organ works[14], Straube showed how ideal phrasing and articulation description of a musical text could look, as previously discussed.

Max Reger seldom took the time to give detailed instructions in his organ works. He often only indicated very long phrasing arcs and provides exact articulations only at very specific points.

A clear insight into Reger's 'phrasing methodology' can be gained by comparing the almost unmarked organ version of the *Chorale Fantasia on 'Freu' dich sehr, o meine Seele!'* Op. 30 with the version for piano four-hands, which was composed at the same time and is characterized with numerous details. The following principles and ideas can be identified in the articulation:

---

[14] Siehe Fußnote 9.

[14] See footnote 9.

1. Alle drei Formen der Riemann-Phrasierung werden verwendet (in-, an- und abbetont):   1) All three forms of Riemann phrasing are used (in-, at- and de-emphasized):

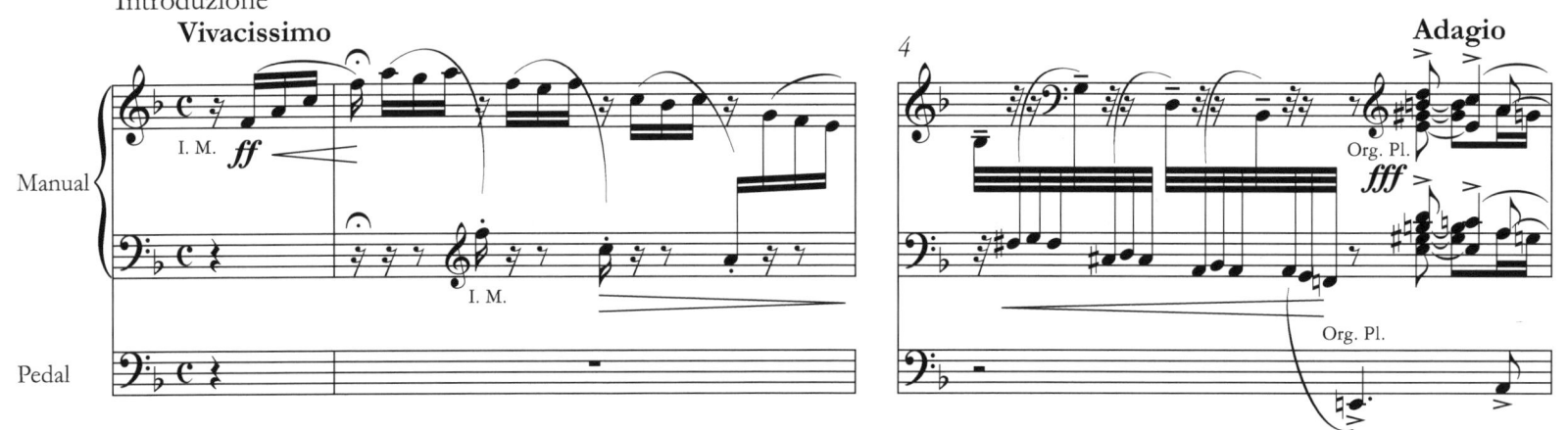

2. Charakteristische, kurze Auftaktgruppen mit unterschiedlicher Abbetonung: 2) Characteristic, short opening groups with different de-emphases:

3. Progressive Gruppen: 3) Progressive groups:

4. Quasi-barocke Takt- / Pulsakzente: 4) Quasi-baroque beat / pulse accents:

5. Ausnahmen: Crescendo-Endbetonung auf Zweiunddreißigstel-Läufen:

5) Exceptions: *crescendo* final accentuation on thirty-second-note runs:

6. Variable Wiederholungsphrasierung:

6) Variable repetition phrasing:

7. Agitato mit kurz abphrasierter Inbetonung: 7) *Agitato* with an in-emphasis and short ending:

8. Variable Auftakte: 8) Variable upbeats:

XVIII

9. Kurze Phrasen bzw. Taktmotive innerhalb des Kontextes langer Phrasen:

9) Short phrases or bar motifs within the context of long phrases:

In Opus 59 setzte Reger drei Arten von Bögen: lange Phrasierungsbögen, Bögen über den Themen ansonsten unbezeichneter, polyphoner Abschnitte und einige wenige kurze Bögen zur Kennzeichnung von charakteristischen Motiven (z. B. Seufzer-Figuren, Scherzo-Passagen).

Karl Straube ergänzte weitere Bögen in folgender Weise:

1. Zwei Ebenen (Architektur/Detail) u. a. zur Gliederung wuchtiger Akkordpassagen: z. B. Nr. 5, T. 10+11 / Nr. 7, T. 13f. / Nr. 7, T. 17ff. / Nr. 7, T. 24–26, 32–34 / Nr. 8, T. 1f. / Nr. 8, T. 44f.

2. Korrektur rein „grifftechnischer" Bögen – linke/rechte Hand – zur Ausdifferenzierung und motivischen Verdeutlichung (z. B. chromatische Linienführung): Nr. 5, T. 11f., 15, 18.

3. Vollständige Bezeichnung/Differenzierung aller Stimmen in langsamen oder polyphonen Abschnitten bzw. Ergänzung unbezeichneter Stellen: Nr. 5, T. 21–25 / Nr. 6 (komplette Bezeichnung aller Fugenstimmen) / Nr. 7, T. 34 (Begleitstimmenphrasierung) / Nr. 8 „Fugato" T. 22ff. Hierbei kommen ähnliche Grundsätze zur Anwendung, wie sie bei Riemann oder Reger (Opus 30) zu konstatieren sind.

4. Häufung von Akzenten in Marcato-Stellen (Marcato-Legato): Nr. 8, T. 1–3 (sowie parallele „Choral-Stellen") / Nr. 8, T. 41f.

In Opus 59, Reger used three types of slurs: long phrasing slurs, slurs over the themes of otherwise unmarked, polyphonic sections and a few short slurs to mark characteristic motifs (e.g. sighing figures, scherzo passages).

Karl Straube added further slurs in the following manner:

1) Two levels (architecture/detail), e.g. for structuring massive chord passages: e.g. No. 5, bars 10+11 / No. 7, bar 13f. / No. 7, bar 17ff. / No. 7, bars 24–26, 32–34 / No. 8, bar 1f. / No. 8, bar 44f.

2) Correction of purely 'technical' fingering slurs – left/right hand – for differentiation and motivic clarification (e.g. chromatic lines): No. 5, bars 11f., 15, 18.

3) Complete marking/differentiation of all parts in slow or polyphonic sections or completion of unmarked passages: No. 5, bars 21–25 / No. 6 (complete marking of all fugue parts) / No. 7, bar 34 (phrasing of accompanying parts) / No. 8 'Fugato' bar 22ff. Similar principles are applied here as in Riemann or Reger (Op. 30).

4) Accumulation of accents in *marcato* passages (*marcato legato*): No. 8, bars 1–3 (as well as parallel 'chorale passages') / No. 8, bar 41f.

Insgesamt verfährt Straube in seinen Ergänzungen eher zurückhaltend unter weitgehender Beibehaltung der von Reger bereits gesetzten Bögen. Seine Zusätze erscheinen häufig ganz im Sinne der Aufführungspraxis, die sich an Riemanns Phrasierung orientiert und zeigen so exemplarisch mögliche Phrasierungs- und Artikulationsfassungen, die ein interpretatorisches Vorbild geben könnten.

Tempo und agogische Gestaltung

Schon Regers Lehrer Hugo Riemann hat die Verbindung von dynamischer und agogischer Gestaltung betont: „Das Hauptgesetz für die dynamische Schattierung der Phrase ist, dass dieselbe stets nur einen Gipfelpunkt hat, bis zu welchem sie *crescendo* hinstrebt und von dem weg sie das *decrescendo* annimmt. [...] Das Gesetz für die agogische Schattierung ist dem entsprechend ein beschleunigter Anschluss der Noten bis zum dynamischen Gipfelpunkt, eine gelinde Dehnung der Schwerpunktnote und, [...] ein allmähliches Abnehmen der Dehnung vom Schwerpunkt zum Ende.“[15] Reger selbst formuliert es in seiner Choralphantasie op. 30 als Fußnote noch kompakter: „doch kann man auch im Tempo bei < etwas *string.* u. bei > etwas *ritard.* (*Tempo rubato*).“[16]

Eine flexible agogische Gestaltung ist demnach zentraler Bestandteil der Interpretation von Regers Werken, dies zeigen auch die Anweisungen Straubes. Dennoch unterscheiden sich Autograf und Bearbeitung in einigen Gesichtspunkten:

Wie in allen Werken der zweiten Weidener „Sturm-und-Drang“-Phase zwischen 1898 und 1900 sind die grundsätzlichen Metronomangaben eher zügig gewählt. Neue Tempoabschnitte werden meistens in Abhängigkeit vom Ausgangstempo mit „Un poco meno mosso“, „Più andante“, „Più mosso“ oder „agitato“ angezeigt (Nr. 5, 7) oder an wenigen zentralen Stellen mit wechselndem Charakter mit einer neuen Metronomzahl versehen (Nr. 8, 9). Insgesamt ergibt sich ein eher einheitliches, verbindendes Tempogefüge mit vereinzelten Abschnitten.

Die Einrichtungen Straubes reduzieren die Tempi erheblich, hier in der Übersicht dargestellt:

Nr. 5	keine Angaben (Reger)	neue M. M. für jeden Abschnitt
Nr. 6	linear (𝅗𝅥 = 56–86)	Gliederung in verschiedene M.M.-Abschnitte ♪ = 92 bis max. ♩ = 76, nicht linear
Nr. 7	keine Angaben	Drei Haupt-M.M.-Ebenen: Grave (♪ = 58–69), Più Andante (♪ = 69–76), Adagio/Largo molto (𝅘𝅥𝅯 = 66–76)
Nr. 8	Con moto festoso 𝅗𝅥 = 72	Maestoso ♩ = 80
	T. 4 a tempo	Con moto ♩ = 96
	T. 7 ---	Maestoso ♩ = 80
	T. 11 a tempo	♩ = 92
	T. 17 ---	Adagio ♩ = 50
	T. 22 Più mosso 𝅗𝅥 = 80	Allegro moderato ♩ = 88

[15] Hugo Riemann, *Vergleichende theoretisch-praktische Klavierschule* op. 39/1, Hamburg 1890, S. 46.
[16] Max Reger, Phantasie über den Choral „Freu' dich sehr, o meine Seele“, München 1899, S. 8.

Overall, Straube proceeds rather cautiously in his additions, largely retaining the slurs already set by Reger. His additions often appear entirely in the spirit of performance practice, which is orientated towards Riemann's phrasing, and thus exemplify possible phrasing and articulation models which could provide an interpretative mould.

Tempo and agogic shaping

Reger's teacher Hugo Riemann already emphasized the connection between dynamic and agogic shading: 'The main law for the dynamic shading of the phrase is that it always has only one climax, to which it strives towards a *crescendo* and from which it assumes a *decrescendo*. [...] The law for the agogic shading is accordingly an accelerated connection of the notes up to the dynamic climax, a slight stretching of the centre note and, [...] a gradual decrease of the stretching from the centre to the end.'[15] Reger himself summarizes this even more succinctly as a footnote in his Chorale Fantasia Op. 30: 'but one can also add some *string.* to the tempo at < and some *ritard.* at > (*Tempo rubato*).'[16]

Flexible agogic organisation is therefore a central component of the interpretation of Reger's works, as Straube's instructions also show. Nevertheless, the autograph and the arrangement differ in some respects:

As in all works from the second Weiden 'Sturm und Drang' phase between 1898 and 1900, the basic metronome markings are rather brisk. New tempo sections are usually indicated as *'Un poco meno mosso'*, *'Più andante'*, *'Più mosso'* or *'agitato'* (Nos. 5, 7), depending on the initial tempo, or a few central passages with a different character are given a new metronome mark (Nos. 8, 9). Overall, the result is a rather uniform, unifying tempo structure with isolated sections.

Straube's indications reduce the speeds considerably, as shown here in the overview:

No. 5	no indications (Reger)	new M. M. for each section
No. 6	linear (𝅗𝅥 = 56–86)	structure in different M.M. sections ♪ = 92 to max. ♩ = 76, not linear
No. 7	no indications	three main M.M. levels: Grave (♪ = 58–69), Più Andante (♪ = 69–76), Adagio/Largo molto (𝅘𝅥𝅯 = 66–76)
No. 8	Con moto festoso 𝅗𝅥 = 72	Maestoso ♩ = 80
	bar 4 a tempo	Con moto ♩ = 96
	bar 7 ---	Maestoso ♩ = 80
	bar 11 a tempo	♩ = 92
	bar 17 ---	Adagio ♩ = 50
	bar 22 Più mosso 𝅗𝅥 = 80	Allegro moderato ♩ = 88

[15] Hugo Riemann, *Vergleichende theoretisch-praktische Klavierschule* Op. 39/1, (Hamburg, 1890), p. 46.
[16] Max Reger, Fantasia on the chorale 'Freu' dich sehr, o meine Seele', (Munich, 1899), p. 8.

	bar 49 Un poco meno mosso 𝅗𝅥 = 76	Andante tranquillo 𝅘𝅥 = 60
	bar 60 Più mosso 𝅗𝅥 = 80	Allegro moderato 𝅘𝅥 = 88
	bar 78 --- Ende rit. in Quasi Adagio	Meno mosso 𝅗𝅥 = 80 Ende rit. zu 𝅗𝅥 = 58
No. 9	Adagio 𝅘𝅥 = 64	Adagio 𝅘𝅥𝅮 = 72
	Vivace assai 𝅗𝅥 = 96	Un poco mosso 𝅗𝅥 = 72–92
	acc. until bar 40 Più vivace 𝅗𝅥 = 130	acc. until bar 35 Più mosso
	rit. T. 46–50, Tempo I 𝅘𝅥𝅮 = 92	rit. T. 40–50 (T. 45 Sostenuto molto, T. 50 Tempo I)

The changes cannot be schematized, for example by reducing them by half. Rather, Straube breaks up Reger's uniform tempo structure into shorter sections in favour of a clear structure, but also at the expense of a continuous build-up of tension.

When Reger continues *accelerandi* up to a climax, even if it is a dense chordal movement, Straube ensures a small-scale structure by calming down and setting fermatas in good time. This principle goes so far in No. 6 that he divides the completely linear ascending fugue into four sections, thus destroying the composer's basic idea.

Overall, Straube favours the order factor. No. 7, bar 35ff. serves as an example of this, in which Straube divides the 'charm' of Reger's somewhat unclear *a tempo / agitato* marking into sections with clear tempo proportions (𝅘𝅥𝅮 = 𝅘𝅥𝅮).

In other pieces, however, the agogic additions also provide further differentiation: in No. 8 Straube sets an accelerated tempo for the upbeats between the chorale-like passages; Straube also considerably slows down chordal intermediate sections, such as in No. 5 or No. 7, thus intensifying the expressive qualities of the passages.

It is therefore necessary to examine in each individual case whether a practical change in performance would lead to an intensification of the expression and message – also in the sense of an intensification corresponding to the numerous reports of Reger's own playing – or whether the exuberant energy of the young composer might be too strongly restrained.

Summary

Karl Straube's performance practice sometimes interferes considerably with Max Reger's original musical text. This affects the most diverse musical parameters. If Reger, possibly due to his almost manic creative urge, often leaves loud dynamic instructions in the ***ff*** range, Straube creates a targeted increase with the help of the free combination and the roll. In terms of agogic design, however, Straube interrupts linear progressions in favour of clear structures in many places. This can be particularly useful in a slow section in order to create pauses in the progression, but it also often inhibits the agogic flow and prevents a move towards the climax.

As Karl Straube had a near monopoly on organ training in Germany in the first half of the 20th century, he was able to establish his style of Reger interpretation as a guideline, even though he fundamentally revised this interpretation after Reger's death, in the course of

Interpretation als Richtschnur etablieren, auch wenn er seine Interpretationsgrundsätze selbst nach Regers Tod im Zuge der Orgelreformbewegung grundlegend überarbeitete. Deshalb ist es notwendig, seine Einrichtungen kritisch zu analysieren. Dennoch bilden sie nach dem originalen Notentext und den Äußerungen Regers zur Aufführungspraxis die Hauptquellen zu Interpretationsfragen des Regerspiels.

Letztendlich gilt es, das Ziel des „seelisch bewegten Vortrags" zu erreichen, den sowohl Reger als auch Straube fordern.

Leipzig, Juni 2024　　　　　　　　　　　　　　　　　　　　　　　　　　*Martin Schmeding*

the organ reform movement. It is therefore necessary to analyse his arrangements critically. Nevertheless, after the original musical text and Reger's comments on performance practice, they form the main sources for questions of interpretation of Reger's works.

Ultimately, the aim is to achieve the 'soulfully moving performance' that both Reger and Straube demand.

Leipzig, June 2024　　　　　　　　　　　　　　　　　　　　　　　　　　*Martin Schmeding*

MAX REGER

ZWÖLF STÜCKE

TWELVE PIECES

Opus 59

Heft 1 / Volume I

1. Praeludium

Max Reger, op. 59, Heft I
(1873–1916)

2. Pastorale

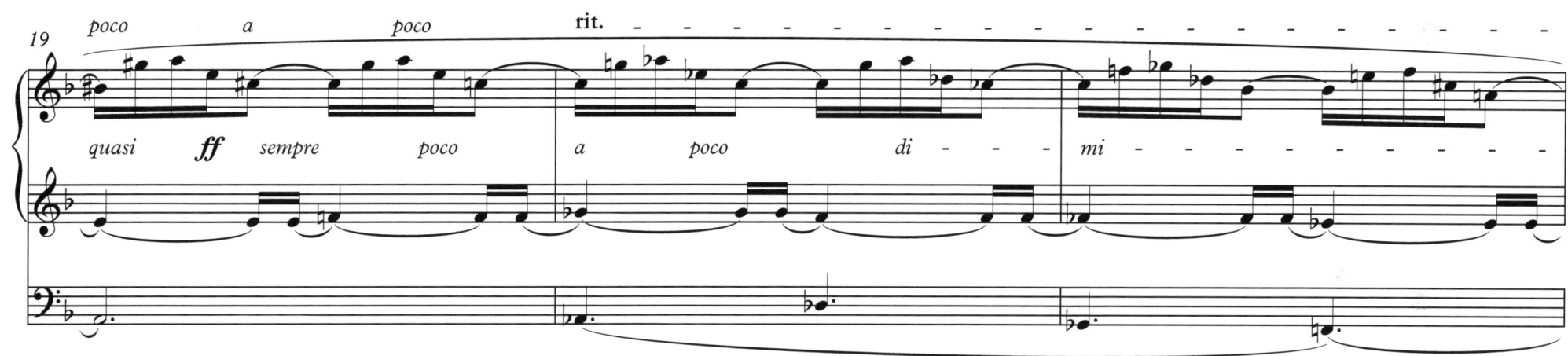
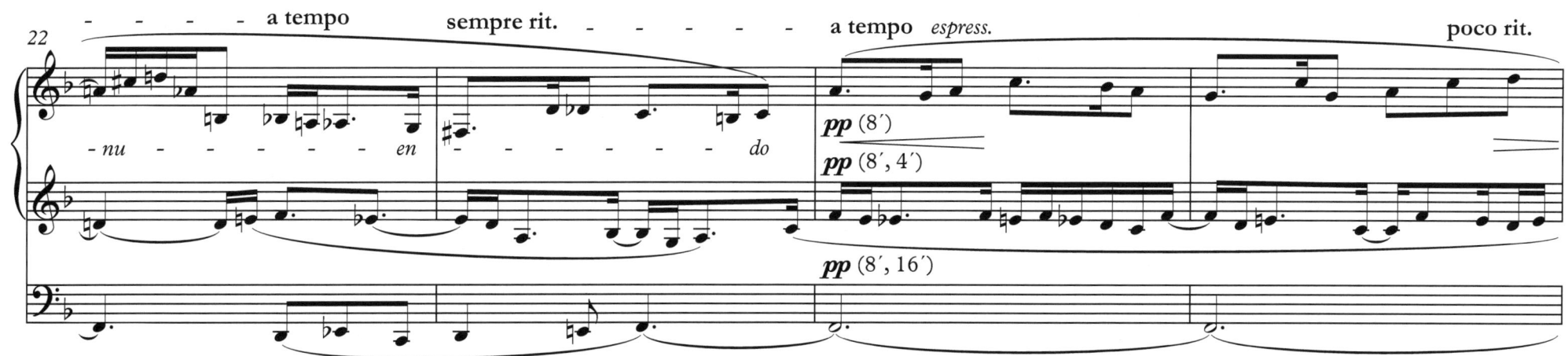

3. Intermezzo

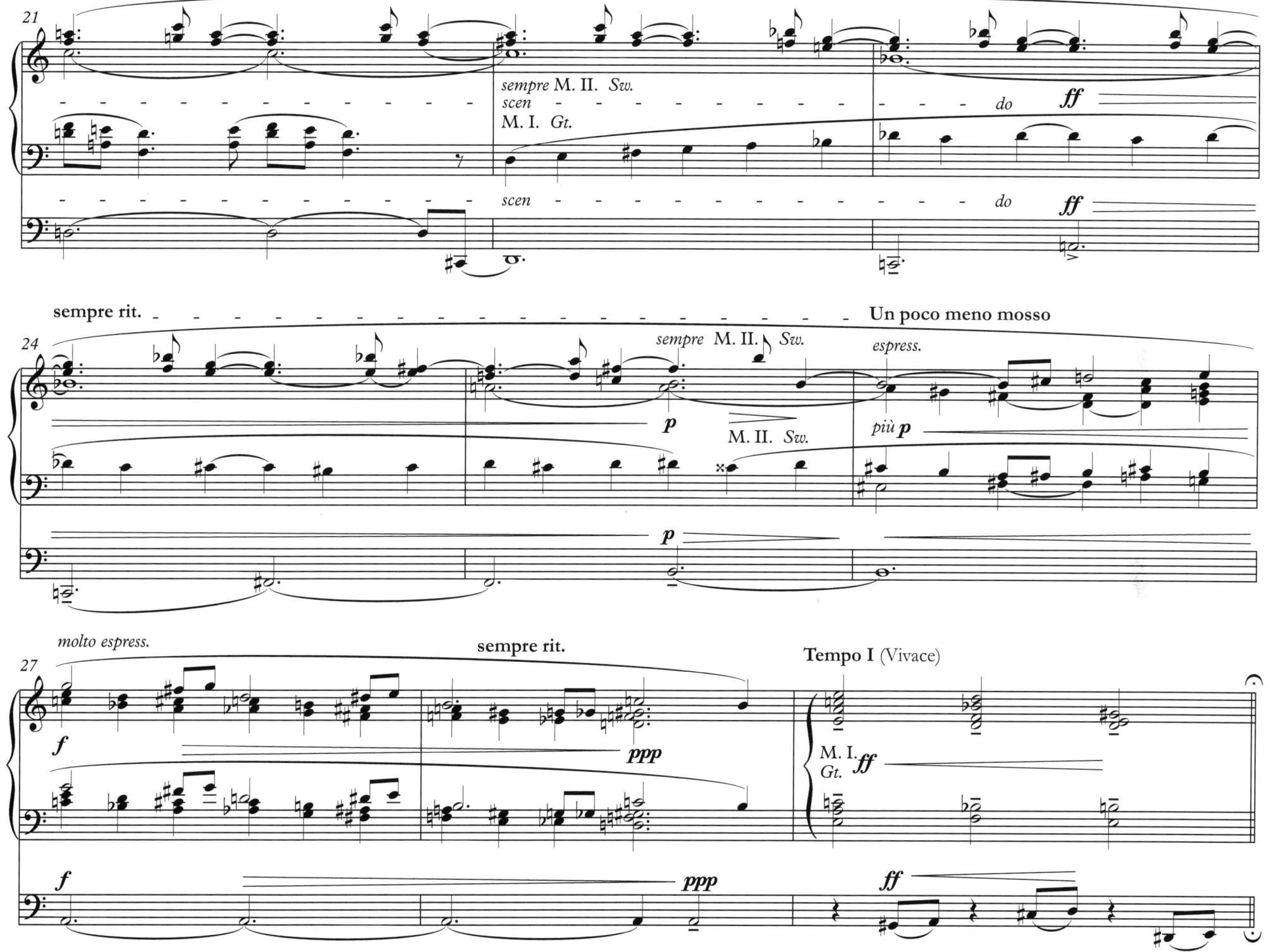

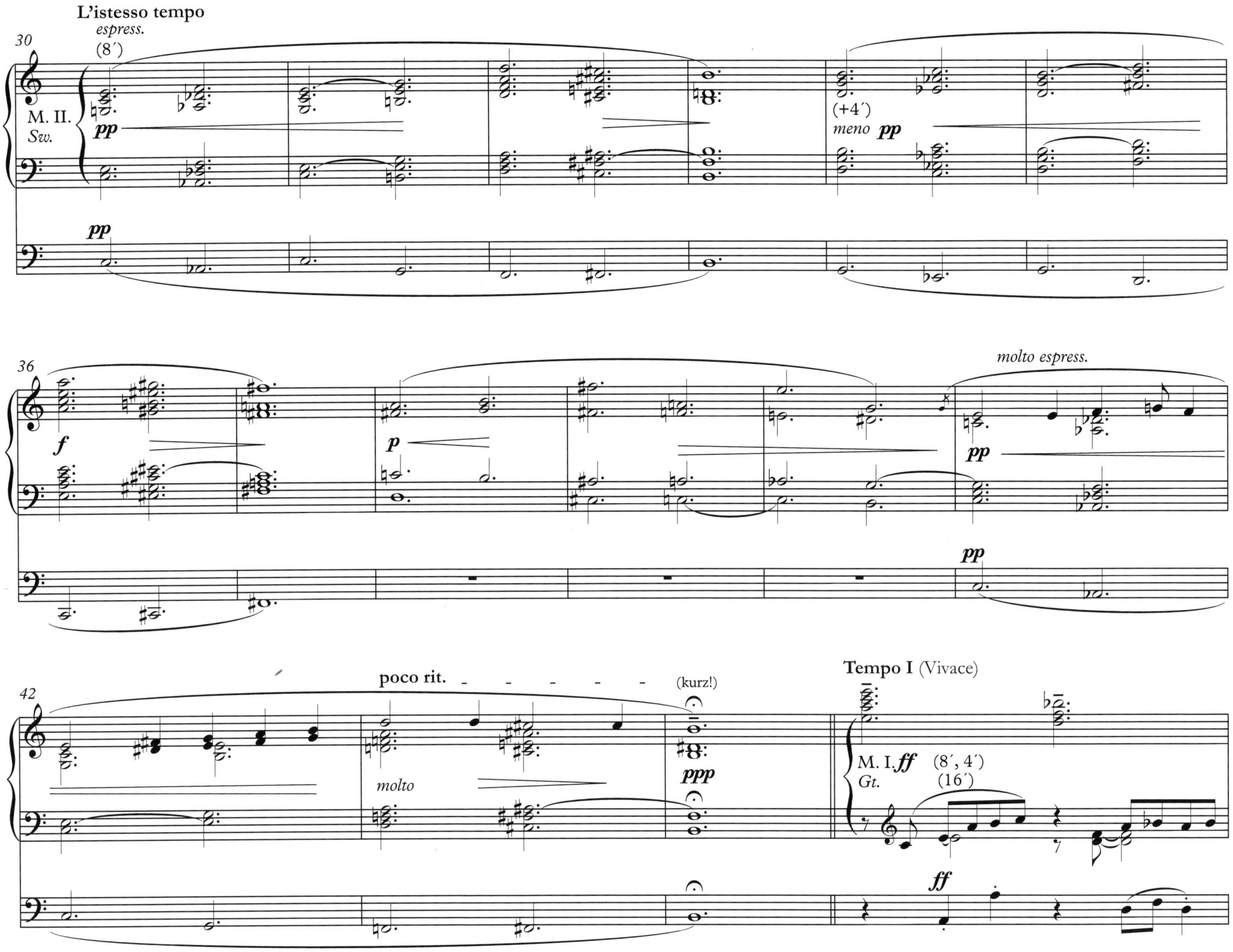
L'istesso tempo
espress.
30
(8´)
M. II.
Sw.
pp
pp
(+4´)
meno pp
36
molto espress.
f
p
pp
pp
42
poco rit.
(kurz!)
molto
ppp
Tempo I (Vivace)
M. I. ff
Gt.
(8´, 4´)
(16´)
ff

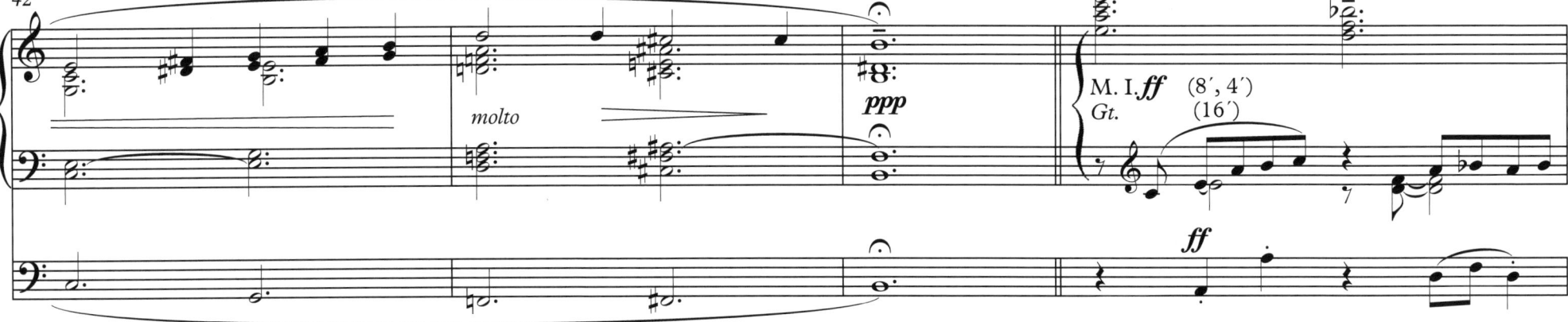

*) Siehe Kritischen Bericht, S. 89. / *See critical commentary, p. 89.*

4. Canon

5. Toccata

6. Fuge

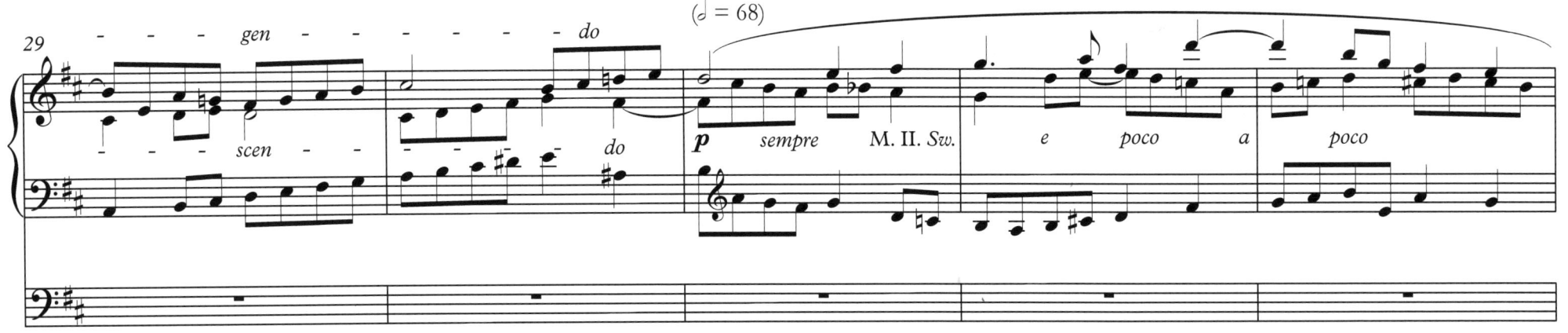

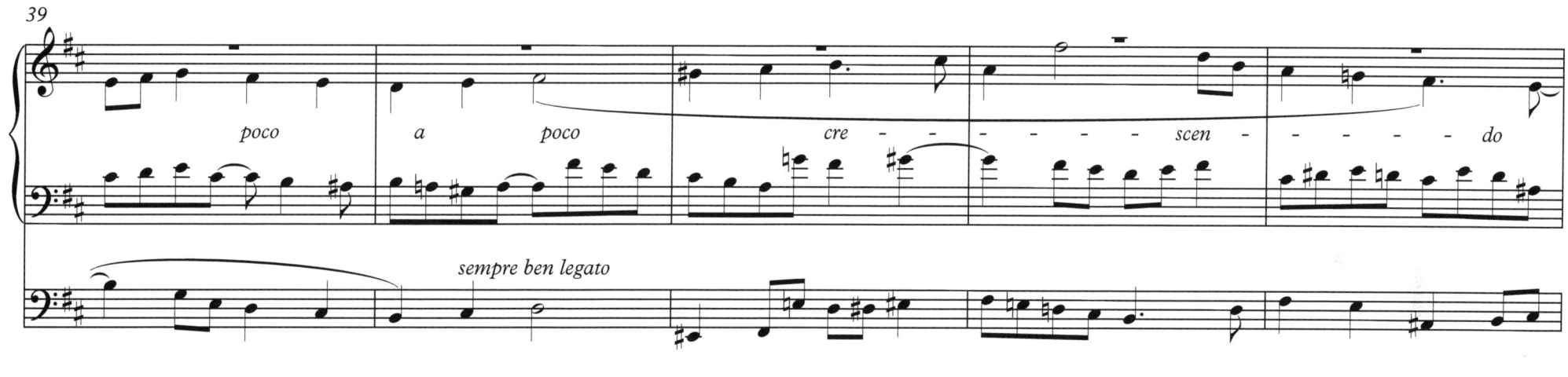

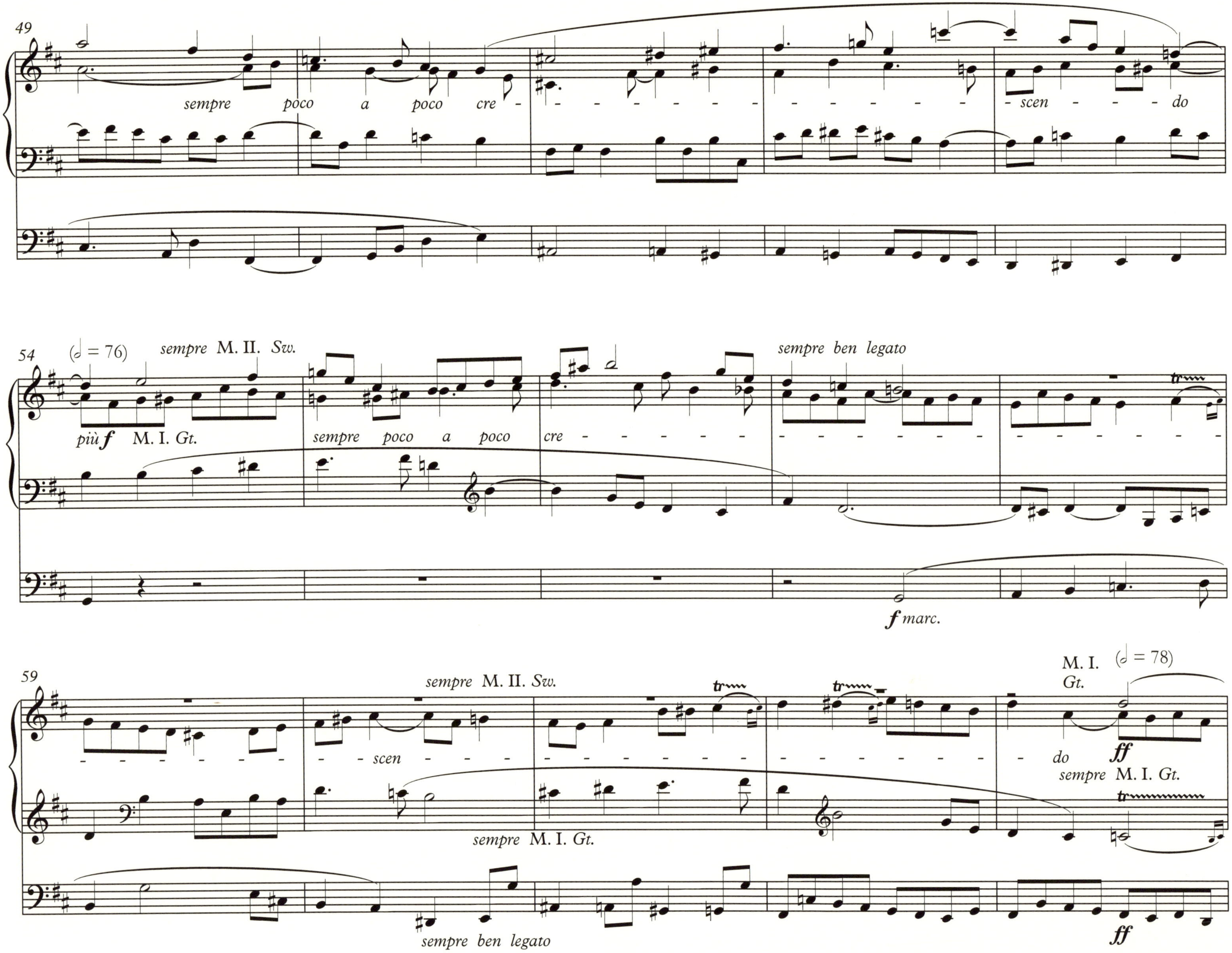
49
sempre poco a poco cre - - - - - - - - - - - - - - - scen - - - do
54
(𝅗𝅥 = 76) sempre M. II. Sw.
sempre ben legato
più f M. I. Gt.
sempre poco a poco cre - - - - - - - - - - - - - - - - - - -
f marc.
59
sempre M. II. Sw.
M. I. Gt. (𝅗𝅥 = 78)
- - - - - - - - scen - do
ff
sempre M. I. Gt.
sempre M. I. Gt.
sempre ben legato
ff

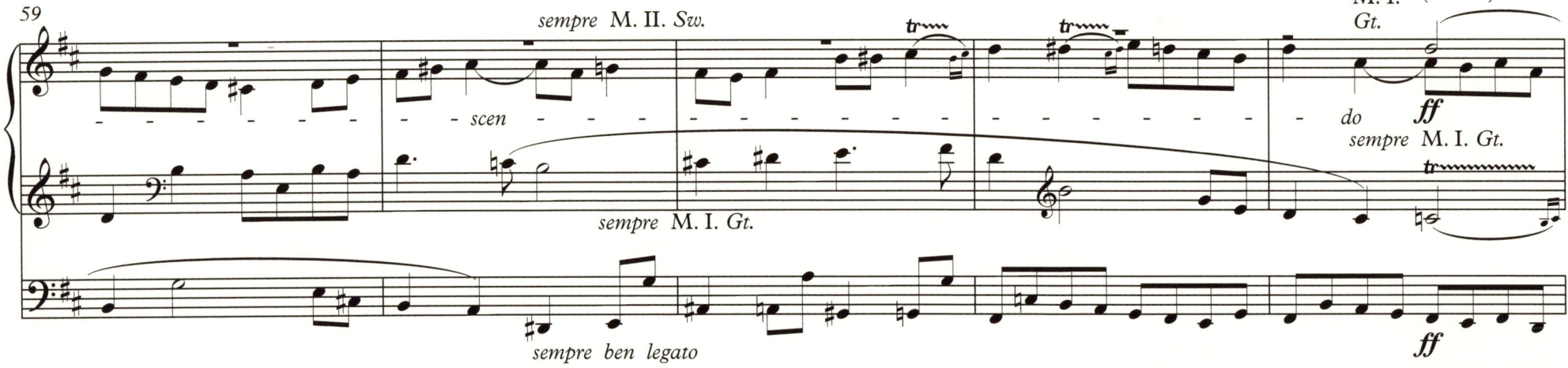

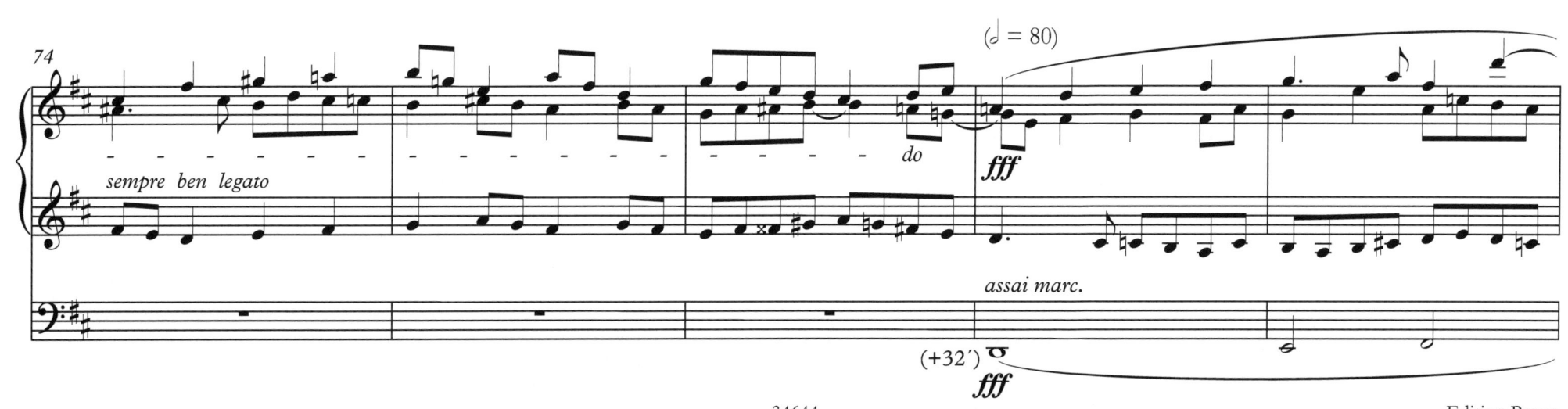

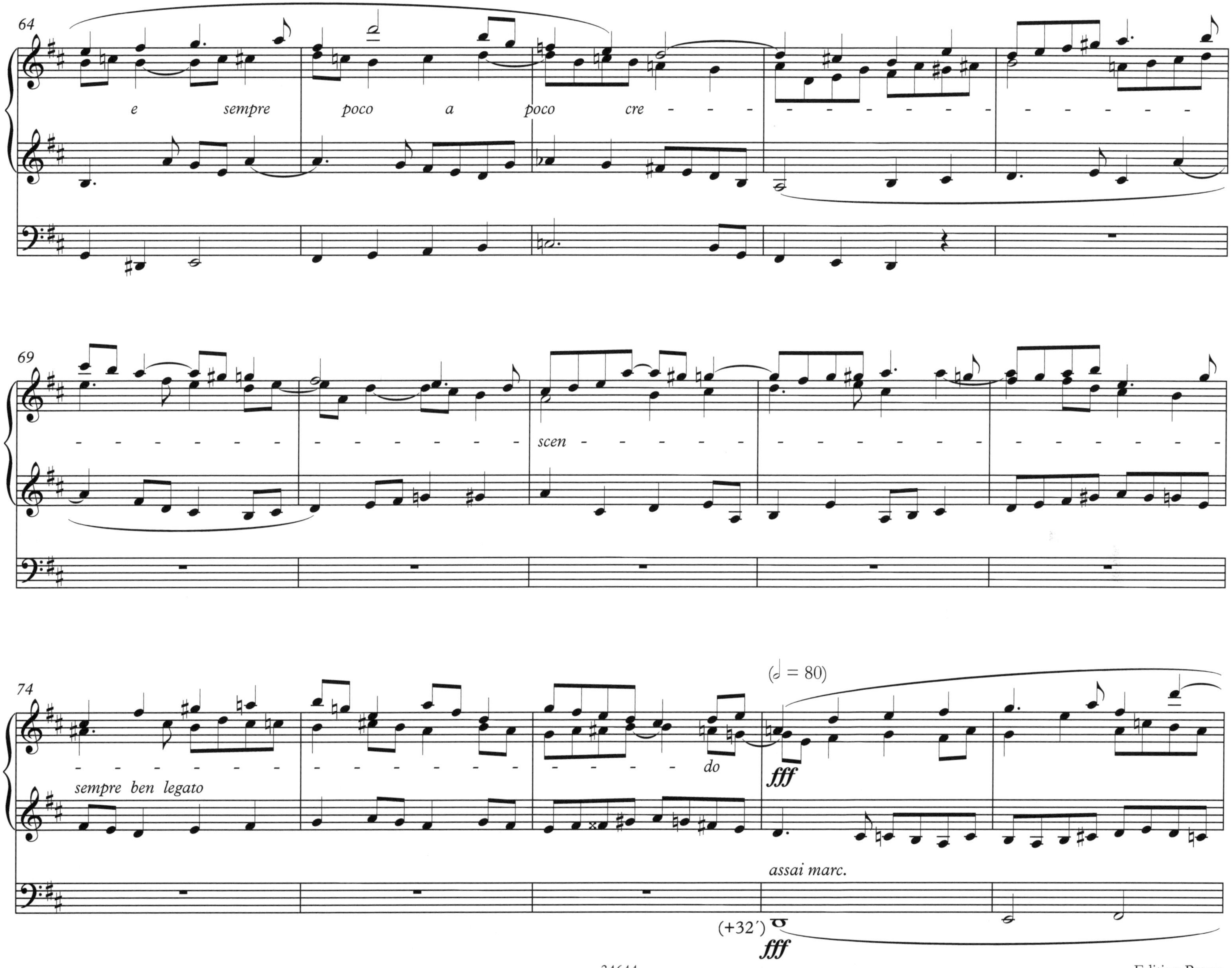
64
e sempre poco a poco cre
69
scen
74
sempre ben legato
do
(𝅗𝅥 = 80)
fff
assai marc.
(+32′)
fff

MAX REGER

ZWÖLF STÜCKE

TWELVE PIECES

Opus 59

Heft 2 / Volume II

7. Kyrie eleison

Max Reger, op. 59, Heft II

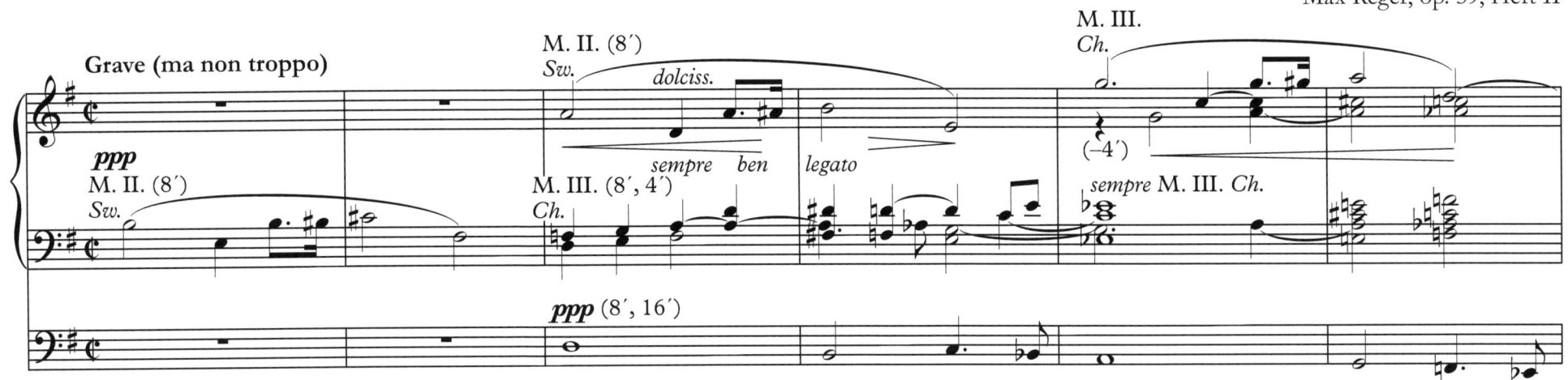

8. Gloria in excelsis

9. Benedictus

10. Capriccio

11. Melodia

12. Te Deum

10
do
ff sempre M. I. Gt.
12
più ff
sempre cre - scen -
15
non rit.
sempre a tempo
do Org. Pl.
M. II. (8′, 4′)
Sw.
mf
sempre
poco a poco cre -

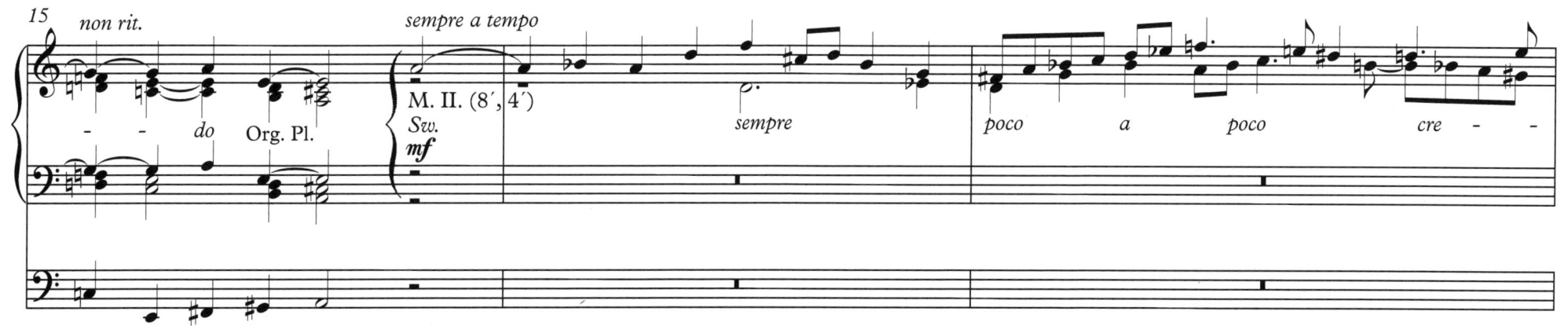

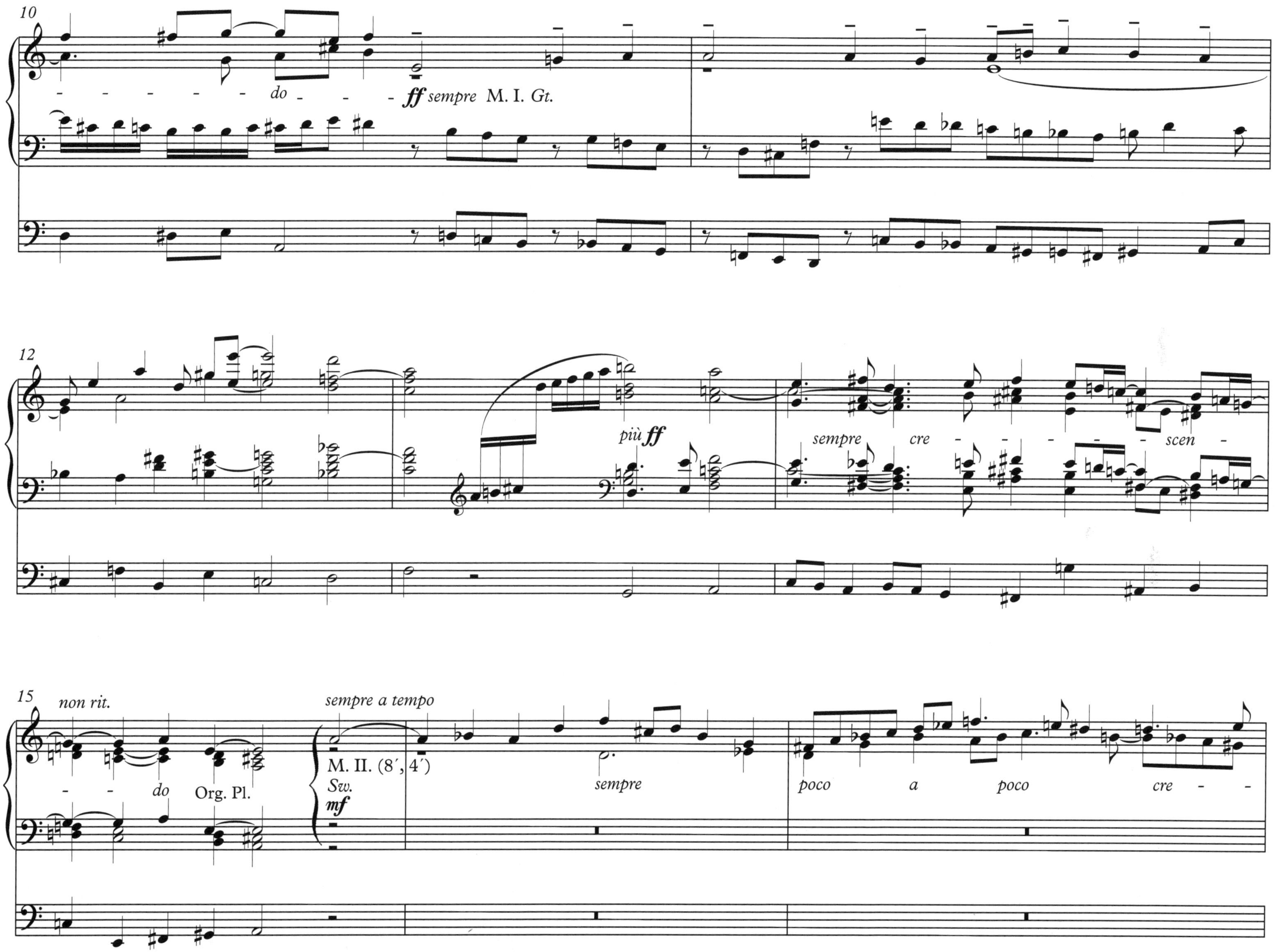

Anhang: Die von Karl Straube eingerichteten Sätze 5–9 /
Appendix: The arranged settings 5–9 by Karl Straube

Toccata und Fuge
Op. 59 Nº 5 und 6.

Handregister.	Erste freie Kombination.	Zweite freie Kombination.		Dritte freie Kombination.

I   Dulciana 8'
    Flauto dolce 8'
    Gemshorn 8'
II Dolce 8'
    Gedackt 8'
    Salicional 8'
    Rohrflöte 8'
III Äoline 8'
    Gedackt 8'
    Gemshorn 8'
    Flûte d'amour 8'
Pedal: Lieblich Gedackt 16'
    Salicetbaß 16'
    Dulciana 8'
M. K. II + I
    III + I
    III + II
P. K. III
	I Flauto dolce 8'
	    Gemshorn 8'
	    Rohrflöte 4'
	    Gemshorn 4'
	II Gedackt 8'
	    Rohrflöte 8'
	    Traversflöte 4'
	    Flageolet 2'
	III Gedackt 8'
	    Gemshorn 8'
	    Flûte d'amour 8'
	    Quintatön 8'
	    Spitzflöte 8'
	    Flauto dolce 4'
	    Flautino 2'
	Pedal: Lieblich Gedackt 16'
	    Salicetbaß 16'
	    Subbaß 16'
	    Dulciana 8'
	    Baßflöte 8'
	    Gemshorn 8'
	M. K. II + I
	    III + I
	    III + II
	P. K. I
	    II
	    III
	Handregister ab.
		I Gemshorn 8'
		    Quintatön 8'
		    Geigenprincipal 8'
		    Gamba 8'
		    Groß-Cymbel 4 fach
		II Dolce 8'
		    Gedackt 8'
		    Salicional 8'
		    Harmonika 8'
		    Cor anglais 8'
		    Salicional 4'
		    Quinte 2⅔'
		    Cornett 3 fach
		III Gedackt 16'
		    Gamba 16'
		    Äoline 8'
		    Voix céleste 8'
		    Gemshorn 8'
		    Flûte d'amour 8'
		    Quintatön 8'
		    Viola 8'
		    Fugara 4'
		    Flautino 2'
		    Harmonia aetheria 3 fach
		    Oboe 8'
		    Trompette harmonique 8'
			Pedal: Untersatz 32'
			    Violon 16'
			    Gemshorn 16'
			    Subbaß 16'
			    Salicetbaß 16'
			    Lieblich Gedackt 16'
			    Cello 8'
			    Gemshorn 8'
			    Baßflöte 8'
			    Dulciana 8'
			    Flauto dolce 4'
			M. K. II + I
			    III + I
			    III + II
			P. K. II
			    III
			Handregister ab.
				II Gedackt 8'
				III Äoline 8'
				    Voix céleste 8
				    Fugara 4'
				    Harmonia aetheria 3 fach
				    Gedackt 16'
				Pedal: Untersatz 32'
				    Salicetbaß 16'
				    Lieblich Gedackt 16'
				    Dulciana 8'
				M. K. II + I
				    III + I
				P. K. I
				    II
				    III
				Handregister ab.

Max Reger.

Edition Peters

Handregister.

I Dulciana 8′	II Dolce 8′	III Äoline 8′	Pedal: Lieblich Gedackt 16′
Flauto dolce 8′	Gedackt 8′	Gedackt 8′	M. K. II + I
Gemshorn 8′	Rohrflöte 8′		III + I
			III + II
			P. K. III

Fuge.
Andante tranquillo. ♪ = 92

Edition Peters

**
 **

Kyrie eleison

Erste freie Kombination

I. Dulciana 8′
Flauto dolce 8′
Quintatön 8′
II. Gedackt 8′
III. Gedackt 8′
Ped. Liebl. Gedackt 16′
Salicetbaß 16′
Gedackt 8′
Dulciana 8′
M.K. II u. I
M.K. III u. I
M.K. III u. II
P. K. III

I. Dulciana 8′
Flauto dolce 8′
Quintatön 8′
II. Dolce 8′
III. Gedackt 16′
Aeoline 8′
Voix céleste 8′
Gedackt 8′
Quinte 2⅔′

Ped. Liebl. Gedackt 16′
Salicetbaß 16′
Dulciana 8′
Gedackt 8′
Untersatz 32′
M.K. II u. I
M.K. III u. I
M.K. III u. II
P. K. III
Handregistrierung für freie
Kombinationen ab

Max Reger, Op. 59 No. 7

Gloria in excelsis

I. Dulciana 8′	II. Dolce 8′	III. Aeoline 8′	Ped. Liebl. Gedackt 16′	M. K. II u. I
Gedackt 8′	Gedackt 8′	Gedackt 8′	Salicetbaß 16′	M. K. III u. I
Flauto dolce 8′	Salicional 8′	Gemshorn 8′	Subbaß 16′	M. K. III u. II
Gemshorn 8′	Rohrflöte 8′	Flûte d'amour 8′	Gemshorn 16′	P. K. I
Quintatön 8′	Harmonika 8′	Quintatön 8′	Violon 16′	P. K. II
Geigenprincipal 8′	Konzertflöte 8′	Spitzflöte 8′	Dulciana 8′	P. K. III
Viola di Gamba 8′	Flauto dolce 4′	Viola 8′	Gemshorn 8′	
Rohrflöte 4′		Traversflöte 4′	Baßflöte 8′	
Gemshorn 4′		Fugara 4′	Cello 8′	

Erste freie Kombination
In allen Manualen 8′ 4′ 2′ Grundstimmen,
gemischte Stimmen, 8′ und 4′ Rohrwerke.
Im Ped. 16′ 8′ 4′ Grundstimmen, 16′ 8′ 4′ Rohrwerke.
Alle Manualkoppeln und Pedalkoppeln.

Zweite freie Kombination
III. Voix céleste 8′
    Fugara 4′
Ped. Gedackt 16′
    Dulciana 8′
P. K. III

Dritte freie Kombination
III. Aeoline 8′
    Gedackt 8′
    Quintatön 8′
    Quinte 2⅔′
Ped. Gedackt 16′
    Salicetbaß 16′
    Dulciana 8′
P. K. III
Für alle drei Kombinationen
Handregistrierung ab.

Op. 59 N° 8

81

Benedictus

Erste freie Kombination

Op. 59, Nr. 9

84

Kritischer Bericht

Critical Commentary

Quellen / Sources

EW Entwürfe
Stadtmuseum Weiden (Max-Reger-Sammlung), Signatur: C 5

Adalbert Lindner hat in einer Mappe die einzelnen Notenblätter mit den Skizzen zu Op. 59 gesammelt und einen Zettel beigefügt: „Diese Mappe enthält sämtliche Skizzen zu […] Op. 59. Es ist das letzte Orgelwerk, das er in Weiden komponierte. In der kurzen Zeit vom 17. Juni bis 1. Juli 1901 wurde es niedergeschrieben, jeden Tag ein fertig abgeschlossenes Stück, das er mir abends vorspielte u. die Skizzen davon zum Geschenk machte." Datierungen von Lindner vgl. Vorwort.

Adalbert Lindner collected the individual sheets of music with the sketches for Op. 59 in a folder and enclosed a note: 'This folder contains all the sketches for […] Op. 59. It is the last organ work he composed in Weiden. It was written down in the short time from 17 June to 1 July 1901, a completed piece every day, which he played to me in the evening and gave me the sketches as a gift.' For dates by Lindner, see preface.

S Stichvorlagen
Heft 1 (Nr. 1–6) und 2 (Nr. 7–12)
Heft 1: Bayerische Staatsbibliothek, München, Signatur; Mus. Ms. 9679
Heft 2: Staatsbibliothek Berlin, Musikabteilung, Signatur: N. Mus. Ms. 668

Titel: *Zwölf Stücke | für die | Orgel | Max Reger, Op. 59 | Heft I*
1.) *Präludium*   4.) *Canon*
2.) *Pastorale*   5.) *Toccata*
3.) *Intermezzo*   6.) *Fuge*

Zwölf Stücke | für die | Orgel | Max Reger, Op. 59 | Heft II
7.) *Kyrie eleison*   10.) *Capriccio*
8.) *Gloria in excelsis Deo*   11.) *Melodia*
9.) *Benedictus, qui venit*   12.) *Te Deum laudamus*
In nomine Domini

Reger verwendete wie üblich schwarze Tinte für den Notentext und rote Tinte für die Vortragsanweisungen. Darüber hinaus weist das Autograph weitere handschriftliche Eintragungen von Verlag, Stecher und Bibliothek auf.

As usual, Reger uses black ink for the musical text and red ink for the performance instructions. In addition, the autograph contains further handwritten entries by the publisher, engraver and library.

Die Manualangaben sind in deutscher und zusätzlich englischer Sprache gehalten:
„I. Man. (Gt.)", „II. Man. (Sw.)", „III. Man. (Ch.)"

The manual entries are in German and also in English:
'I. Man. (Gt.)', 'II. Man. (Sw.)', 'III. man. (Ch.)'

Bei folgenden Satzangaben wurden Teile gestrichen: Nr. 8 Deo, Nr. 9 qui venit in nomine Domini, Nr. 12 laudamus.

Parts of the following movements have been deleted: No. 8 Deo, No. 9 qui venit in nomine Domini, No. 12 laudamus.

E Erstdruck Verlag C. F. Peters, Leipzig, September 1901,
Heft 1: EP 3008a, Plattennummer 8757
Heft 2: EP 3008b, Plattennummer 8758

Titel: *Zwölf Stücke | für die Orgel | MAX REGER | Op. 59. | Aufführungsrecht vorbehalten. | Eigenthum des Verlegers. | 8757./8758. | LEIPZIG | C. F. PETERS*

Ab 1903 erschienen bis 1918 sieben weitere Auflagen. Das Copyright wurde 1929 erneuert. Nr. 9 wurde zwischen 1910 und 1918 in drei Einzelauflagen veröffentlicht.

Since 1903 seven further editions were published from 1903 until 1918. The copyright was renewed in 1929. No. 9 was published in three separate editions between 1910 and 1918.

Die Manualangaben sind in deutscher und zusätzlich englischer Sprache gehalten:
„I. Man. (Gt.)", „II. Man. (Sw.)", „III. Man. (Ch.)"

The manual details are in German and also in English:
'I. Man. (Gt.)', 'II. Man. (Sw.)', 'III. Man. (Ch.)'

H Erstdruck der Harmoniumfassung von Nr. 9, C. F. Peters, Leipzig, September 1908.
EP 3215, Plattennummern 9337.

Titel: *Benedictus | für Harmonium | von | MAX REGER | Opus 59 No. 9. | Aufführungsrecht vorbehalten. | Eigentum des Verlegers. | 9337. | LEIPZIG | C. F. PETERS*

Die Neuedition verwendet den Erstdruck als Leitquelle, als Vergleich wird die Stichvorlage hinzugezogen. Die Skizzen sind sehr rudimentär gehalten und halten die meisten Elemente nur in graphischer Kurzschrift fest, können deshalb kaum zur Erstellung des Notentextes einbezogen werden. Auch die Harmonium-Fassung wurde nur um unwesentliche Elemente in den Aufführungsanweisungen ergänzt.

The new edition uses the first edition as its main source, and the engraver's model is consulted for comparison. The sketches are very rudimentary and only record most of the elements in graphic shorthand and can therefore hardly be used to create the musical text. The harmonium version also only adds insignificant elements to the performance instructions.

Für die aufführungspraktischen Betrachtungen wird eingehend Bezug auf die beiden Einrichtungen Karl Straubes einzelner Nummern aus Opus 59 genommen: Nr. 7–9 aus dem Jahr 1912, Nr. 5–6 von 1919.

For the practical performance considerations, detailed reference is made to Karl Straube's two arrangements of individual numbers from Opus 59: Nos. 7–9 from 1912, Nos. 5–6 from 1919.

Praktische Ausgabe von Karl Straube 1912
Verlag C. F. Peters, Leipzig, 1912 (Nr. 7–9), Plattennummer 9683.

Titel: wie **E**; mit Vermerk: *Hieraus: Kyrie eleison, Gloria in excelsis und Benedictus | Im Einverständnis mit dem Komponisten herausgegeben von KARL STRAUBE.*

Eine persönliche Übergabe von Korrekturen an den Verleger Henri Hinrichsen vom 10. Juli 1912 (vgl. Susanne Popp und Susanne Shigihara (Hg.), *Max Reger.*

A personal delivery of corrections to the publisher Henri Hinrichsen dated 10 July 1912 (cf. Susanne Popp and Susanne Shigihara (eds.), *Max Reger. Briefwechsel mit*

Briefwechsel mit dem Verlag C. F. Peters, Bonn 1995, S. 485) legt nahe, dass Max Reger mit Straubes Einrichtung vertraut war – inwiefern er diese trotz der essentiellen Veränderungen auch unterstützte, ist nicht bekannt.

Kurz nach Regers Tod erschienen noch die beiden Stücke Nr. 5 und 6 in einem Sammelband von Präludien und Fugen in Straubes Bearbeitung.

dem Verlag C. F. Peters, Bonn 1995, p. 485) suggests that Max Reger was familiar with Straube's arrangement – the extent to which he supported it despite the essential changes is not known. Shortly after Reger's death, the two pieces Nos. 5 and 6 were published in an anthology of preludes and fugues in Straube's arrangements.

Praktische Ausgabe von Karl Straube 1919
Verlag C. F. Peters, Leipzig, 1919 (Nr 5+6), Plattennummer 10036.

Titel: *Präludien und Fugen | für die Orgel | von | MAX REGER | herausgegeben | von | KARL STRAUBE. | Aufführungsrecht vorbehalten. | Eigentum des Verlegers. | LEIPZIG | C. F. Peters | 10036.*

Straube richtete insgesamt 10 Paare von Präludien und Fugen (bzw. Toccata oder Improvisation und Fuge) aus op. 59, 65, 80 und 85 vermutlich für den praktischen Gebrauch, v. a. im Orgelunterricht am Konservatorium ein, darunter zu Beginn Op. 59, Nr. 5–6 Toccata d-Moll und Fuge D-Dur.

Straube arranged a total of 10 pairs of preludes and fugues (or toccata or improvisation and fugue) from Op. 59, 65, 80 and 85 presumably for practical use, especially in organ lessons at the conservatory, including at the beginning Op. 59, Nos. 5–6 Toccata in D minor and Fugue in D major.

Einzelbemerkungen

Abkürzungen:
Ped. = Pedal
r.H./l.H. = rechte Hand/linke Hand
T. = Takt
Zz = Zählzeit
Zitierfolge: Taktzahl – r.H./l.H./Ped. – Zeichen (Noten und Pausen) – Quelle (siehe Quellen/Sources) – Lesart der genannten Quelle bzw. Bemerkung

1. Präludium

2 r.H. **E** Oberstimme 1 Bogen nur bis zum ersten Nachschlagston, in **S** unklar (evtl. Lesefehler)
6 r.H. **S** Oberstimme 4 ohne tenuto-Strich, *poco rit.* mit Fortführungsstrichen bis (kurz!)
9 Ped. **S** 1 Kommentar: Klein das ♮ zu ♮
13 r.H. **E** Unterstimme 5 ohne Staccato-Punkt
15 l.H. **S, E** 10 ohne Staccato-Punkt, wird in der Ausgabe ergänzt, da im Umfeld alle Parallelstellen gleiche Artikulationsangaben aufweisen
17 Man. **S** ab Zz 4+ *sempre fff*
18 r.H. **E** 9 Viertelhals nur für *dis²*
27 r.H. **S** 1 Bogenende unklar, evtl. bis Zz 2
28 r.H. **S** Bogenende unklar (zwischen Oberstimme 4 und Unterstimme 8)
30 r.H. **E** Unterstimme 9 Bogenende auf erstem Nachschlagston
31 r.H. **E** Zz 5 Viertelhals nur für *gis¹*
35 l.H. **E** Zz 6 Akkord mit *ais¹*
38 Man. **E** Zz 4 Viertelhals nur für die jeweilige Oberstimme (*fis²* bzw. *e¹*)
38 r.H. **S** Oberstimme 8–9 Bogenende unklar
38 Ped. **E** 7 bis T. 39,1 ohne Bogen
39 r.H. **E** Zz 2 Viertelhals nur für Oberstimme
39 l.H. **E** Zz 1 Viertelhals nur für Unterstimme
47 r.H. **E** Zz 3+ Achtelhals nur für *gis¹*
48 l.H. **S** Zz 6 Oberstimme Sechzehntel *fis¹–gis¹*
49 Man. **E** Zz 6+ Achtelhals nur für die jeweilige Oberstimme
50 Man. **E** Zz 6 Viertelhals nur für die jeweilige Oberstimme

2. Pastorale

37 Ped. **S** Decrescendo-Gabel erst ab Zz 2
38 Man. **E** Decrescendo-Gabel erst auf dem Schlussakkord, wahrscheinlich bedingt durch die Ausdehnung der Dynamikangabe ***ppp***, Ausgabe folgt **S**

3. Intermezzo

9 r.H. **E** 1 Achtelhals nur für Oberstimme (*g¹*)
9 Ped. **S** 1 Fortführungsstriche bis Zz 2
10 l.H. **E** Zz 4 Viertelhals nur für *e¹*
21 r.H. **S** Zz 6 ohne Bogen *f²* zu *fis²* (T. 22,1)
23 **S** Decrescendo-Gabel erst ab Zz 5+
25 Ped. **S** Decrescendo-Gabel erst ab Zz 5
44 r.H. **S** 1 ohne Tenuto-Strich
44 Man. **E** Dynamikangabe ***p***
49 r.H. **S** Kommentar: Bitte genau so stechen; Alternativ-Version für Orgeln mit kleinerem Manualumfang

4. Canon

15 Man. **E** Crescendo endet bei Zz 2+, Ausgabe folgt **S**
16 r.H. **S, E** Zz 3 Registrierungsangabe (sempre 4′) erscheint nicht logisch, da bisher nur mit 8′ registriert wurde, evtl. Schreibfehler, dann müsste es (sempre 8′) heißen

21 r.H. **S** Bogenanfang unklar, zwischen 8 und 9
23 r.H. **E** *poco a poco rit.* ohne Fortführungsstriche, Ausgabe folgt **S**

5. Toccata

3 r.H. **S** Zz 2 ohne Bogen zur Vorschlagsnote
11 l.H. **E** Zz 2+ *b* ohne Achtelhals
20 Man. **E** Crescendo ohne Fortführungsstriche bis Org. Pl., Ausgabe folgt **S**
24 l.H. **S** Oberstimme Zz 4 *d¹*
28 l.H. **S** 6–7 ohne Haltebogen
29 Man. **S** 2 Kommentar: Die [Arpeggien] ganz durch!
30 l.H./r.H. **S** Oberstimme zwei Achtel
33 r.H. **E** *stringendo* ohne Fortführungsstriche bis *a tempo*, Ausgabe folgt **S**
37 Man. **E** *molto rit.* ohne Fortführungsstriche, Ausgabe folgt **S**

6. Fuge

25 r.H. **E** Unterstimme ohne Bogen bis T. 27, Zz 4, Ausgabe folgt **S**, da alle Themeneinsätze mit Bogen versehen sind
39 Man. **S** Taktmitte erstes *poco* fehlt
40 r.H. **S** Taktmitte schon hier Metronomangabe ♩ = 74, wohl aus Versehen stehengeblieben, weil die Anweisung in T. 44 noch einmal steht
64 Ped. **S** 3 Bogen bis T. 67,3
66 r.H. **S** Bogen bis Oberstimme 3
66 r.H. **S** Unterstimme 3 ohne ♮
86 r.H. **E** Unterstimme 1 *a¹* ohne Viertelhals
90 l.H. **S** Bogen endet Zz 3

7. Kyrie eleison

4 l.H. **E** Oberstimme Zz 4 c^1 ohne Viertelhals
14 Man. **S** Fortführungsstriche *cresc.* bis Taktende
15 l.H. **S, E** Registerangabe erst Zz 2+
17 r.H. **E** Zz 1 d^2 ohne Viertelhals
17 r.H. **E** Zz 3 e^2 ohne Viertelhals mit Punkt (falscher Rhythmus)
22 r.H. **E** Oberstimme Zz 4 *gis* ohne Viertelhals
31 r.H. **E** Oberstimme Zz 1+3 ohne Viertelhals

8. Gloria in excelsis

Titel **S** „Deo" ausgestrichen
11 r.H. **E** *rit.* ohne Fortführungsstriche bis Zz 3
11 l.H. **E** *crescendo* ohne Fortführungsstriche bis Zz 3
16 Man. **E** *crescendo* ohne Fortführungsstriche bis ***fff***
31 l.H. **S** 7 g^1
41 r.H. **E** Unterstimme a^1 ohne Viertelhals
45 r.H. **E** Unterstimme Zz 4 d^1 ohne Viertelhals
47 r.H. **E** Unterstimme Zz 2 g^1 ohne Viertelhals
48 r.H. **E** e^2 ohne Punkt
53 r.H. **S, E** Oberstimme 4–5 Trillernachschlag ohne Vorzeichen, in Ausgabe aus harmonischen Gründen ergänzt
59 r.H. **E** *rit.* Fortführungsstriche nur bis Anfang T. 60

9. Benedictus

Titel **S** „qui venit in nomine Domini" ausgestrichen
1 Man. **H** Dynamikangabe ***pp***
2 Man. **H** Crescendo-Gabel ab Taktmitte bis T. 3, Zz 2
3 l.H. **E** 2 Viertelhals nur für b^1; **H** es^1 ohne Haltebogen zu Zz 3
5 Man. **H** Dynamikangabe ***pp***
7 Man. **H** Dynamikangabe ***f***
7 Man. **H** Zz 3 Decrescendo-Gabel bis 9, Zz 3+ ***pp***
8 Man. **H** Zz 3 (+4′)
11 Man. **H** 1 Crescendo mit Fortführungsstrichen und Crescendo-Gabel bis T. 12,1
12 r.H. **E** *molto rit.* ohne Fortführungsstriche
18 l.H. **E** Oberstimme Zz 4 es^1 ohne Viertelhals
24 r.H. **H** Taktmitte Tempoangabe *Più mosso* (♩ = 96), Registrierung (+8′+4′)
28 r.H. **H** 3 Bogen bis T. 40,2
41 **H** Tempoangabe (♩ = 144)
45 Man. **E** *crescendo* nur bis Zz 3
48 r.H. **E** *rit.* Fortführungsstriche nur bis Taktende
51 l.H. **E** Unterstimme Zz 2 es^1 ohne Viertelhals
54 Man. **H** Zz 3 Dynamikangabe ***pp***

10. Capriccio

30 l.H. **S, E** 7–9 ohne Bogen; als Herausgeberzusatz ergänzt
72 Ped. **E** 4 tenuto-Strich
73 r.H. **S** Kommentar: Genauso mit [ ] für *ais*

11. Melodia

13 r.H. **E** *poco rit.* ohne Fortführungsstriche
22 r.H. **S** *agitato e sempre molto* (danach fehlt weiteres Wort)
23 r.H. **S** 8 Decrescendo-Gabel beginnt schon hier
40 r.H. **S** Decrescendo-Gabel schon ab Zz 2

12. Te Deum

Titel **S** „laudamus" ausgestrichen
3 r.H. **E** Oberstimme 1 ohne Achtelhals; Ausgabe folgt **S** aus rhythmischen Gründen
3 r.H. **E** Oberstimme 6 Viertelhals nur für b^1
10 Man. **E** *crescendo* ohne Fortführungsstriche bis ***ff***
15 r.H. **S, E** Unterstimme 2–3 gehaltene Viertelnote c^1–e^1 statt Halbenote (l.H.), in **EW** separate Viertelnote
23 r.H. **E** *poco rit.* ohne Fortführungsstriche
23 Man. **E** *crescendo* ohne Fortführungsstriche
25 r.H. **E** *rit.* ohne Fortführungsstriche
34 **S** Taktmitte Kommentar: „2. Halben Takt siehe nächste Seite (24)"

ISMN 979-0-014-13513-3